THEY CAME FROM AFAR

First impression: 2023

© Copyright John Aitchison, 2023

The contents of this book are subject to copyright, and may not be reproduced by any means, mechanical or electronic, without the prior, written consent of the publishers.

Cover design: Y Lolfa

Most images are from the author's private collection. Every effort has been made to trace the creators of the other images. In some cases, this has not been possible. If you are aware of any infringement of copyright please contact the author jwaitchison@hotmail.com.

ISBN: 978 1 80099 405 8

Published and printed in Wales
on paper from well-maintained forests by
Y Lolfa Cyf., Talybont, Ceredigion SY24 5HE
website www.ylolfa.com
e-mail ylolfa@ylolfa.com
tel 01970 832 304
fax 832 782

THEY CAME FROM AFAR

BIOGRAPHICAL SKETCHES

ANTIBES, JUAN-LES-PINS
AND CAP D'ANTIBES

JOHN AITCHISON

*For
Jonathan
(1973-2022)
In memoriam*

Contents

	Introduction	11
1	Antibes, Juan-les-Pins and Cap d'Antibes	15
2	Villa Eilenroc: Family Sagas	59
3	Villa Soleil, Grand Hôtel du Cap and Château des Enfants	105
4	Russians and Montenegrins in Exile	135
5	Oligarchs: Rise and Retreat	163
	Notes	189
	General References	197

Liégeard : Côte d'Azur 1887
Gallica.bnf.fr

Cap d'Antibes

Antibes

'Tout ici rayonne, tout fleurit, tout chante. Le soleil, la femme, l'amour sont là chez eux. J'en ai encore le resplendissement dans les yeux et dans l'âme...

Victor Hugo: *'Hommage de la Ville d'Antibes'*

Juan-les-Pins

'le Balcon Fleuri'
'le Mecque du Bonheur'

Le Cap d'Antibes

'The peninsula is a rare combination of trees and rocks and winding roads, almost surrounded by the pulsing Mediterranean, always cool and comfortable even in summer, and scarcely ever troubled by the blowing of the mistral. Villas, almost without end, occupy the Cap, tree-hidden, and brilliantly stuccoed (sic) with a tint which so well harmonizes with surrounding tropical flora that the effect is of a fairy-land.'

Francis Miltoun: *'Rambles in Provence and on the Riviera', 1907*

Introduction

'From Avignon, the south is felt and seen. For a person who has always lived in the north, the first encounter with southern nature is filled with solemn joy – you become young, you want to sing, to dance, to weep: everything is so brilliant, gay and luxurious.'

Alexander Herzen, *'Letters from France and Italy'*, December 1847.

In 1887 Stéphen Liégeard, a political figure, poet, historian, administrator and travel writer of some repute, famously described the Mediterranean stretch of coast, from Marseille in the west to Genoa in the east, as *La Côte d'Azur*. At the time, his dense, ornately written and richly illustrated guide to the area was widely acclaimed; so much so in fact that it was deemed worthy of the *Prix Bordin* – a prestigious literary award bestowed by the *Institut de France (Académie des Sciences Morales)*. At a public gathering to mark its publication, the academician Camille Doucet said of *'this charming book'*, that it captured the wondrous nature of the coast, and in a manner that was as *'colourful and bright as the azure scenes that it depicted'*.

As for Liégeard himself, he saw the whole coastal zone as a strand *'of light, of warm breezes and of secret, fragrant forests'*; one that was *'blessed'* and *'delicious in its entirety'*. His panegyric, penned during the halcyon days of the *Belle Époque*, not only enthused over the region's natural allure, its suite of coastal settlements, its rural interior (*l'arrière pays*), together with its multi-layered cultural heritage, it also introduced the reader to a host of notable personalities and

Stéphen Liégeard

families who, over the years, and in very different ways, had helped to shape the development of the littoral, and ultimately to establish its international reputation as a highly fashionable and very select place of resort and residence. Now, for the first time, the coast had a suitably resonant name to capture and attract foreign imaginations. The simple descriptor *'La Côte d'Azur'* would soon come to enfold a seductive myth of international renown – an Edenic suffusion of sea, sun, sky and scenery. Here, bathed in a cerulean sky, there was much to distract and enliven even the most jaded of spirits.

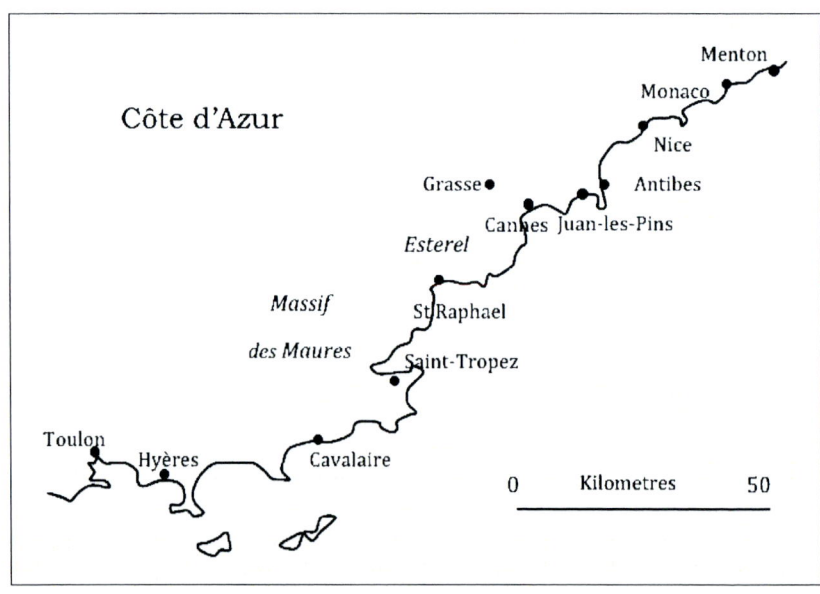

La Côte d'Azur

Adding greatly to the allure of the coastal scene is a long series of promontories, which, together with their associated coves and bays, ascribe indented variety. It is with just one of these capes that this study is specifically concerned – Cap d'Antibes, together with the two adjoining 'gateway' towns of Antibes and Juan-les-Pins.

The five essays that follow are freestanding and largely biographical in nature. In the main, they focus on particular people, in particular places and at particular periods of time. As to the latter, the emphasis is on the *Belle Époque* and '*Les Années Folles*' (The Crazy Years). However, where deemed appropriate, reference is made to both earlier and much more recent times. To add further depth, at various points wider social, economic and political contexts are also broached.

Finally, it will be readily apparent to the reader that the great majority of those who figure most prominently arrived in the locality from foreign parts. Hence the overarching title of the text: 'They Came From Afar'.

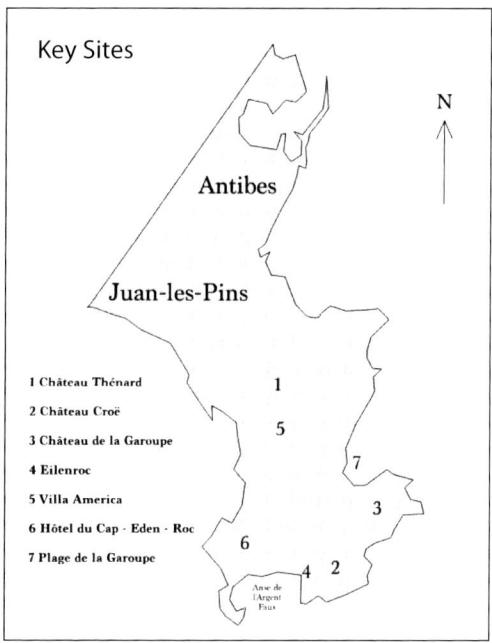

1
Antibes, Juan-les-Pins and Cap d'Antibes

Antibes first came to the fore as a Greek trading post (named Antipolis) in the 4th century BC, and then as a site of Roman settlement. Over the centuries that followed, Antiboul, as it was long called, was but a small port town serving the commercial needs of the local agricultural and fishing community. Following the union of that part of Provence, later to be known as the County of Nice, with the Duchy of Savoy in 1386, the settlement was suddenly transmuted into a border garrison of considerable strategic and military significance. This was especially the case when its region – Provence – was formally bequeathed to Louis XI of France. During the 16th century and then, more significantly, during the last decade of the 17th century (following designs by the famed military engineer, Sébastien Vauban), the settlement was enclosed by ramparts, walls and bastions; further fortifications were also constructed around the port, including the imposing *Fort Carré*, located at the entrance to the wide but relatively small and ill-equipped harbour.

Antibes was to remain locked in the embrace of this heavy stone girdle for a further two centuries. Sited just a dozen or so kilometres from the frontier with the Kingdom of Piedmont-Sardinia, the town maintained its military purpose, but at the same time continued to operate as a regional marketplace, coastal

Fort Carré and Port Vauban

trading hub and ecclesiastic centre. More and more arrivals to the town came with a view to either stopping over, or simply moving on, perhaps to Genoa or to Marseille, by felucca or other craft.

At the time, what would later become Juan-les-Pins was a mere hamlet with very limited facilities. It could hardly be called a settlement, and was mainly a place that attracted weekend excursionists from nearby Antibes and its immediate environs. A scattering of bathing huts along the curve of sandy beaches overlooking *La Baie de Golfe Juan*, together with sites for picnicking amidst fragrant pine groves, attracted mostly day-trippers. Retail outlets were as a consequence meagre in the extreme. Needless to say, the place certainly had little, if anything, to attract visitors from away. The situation would change, however, with the coming of the mainline railway in the early 1860s, but relatively few in number were those who would consider stopping off.

Whilst Antibes itself may not have welcomed all that many visitors, beyond its ramparts the countryside around, including Cap d'Antibes, had much to delight the senses. In 1763 when on his way to Nice, even the ever critical Tobias Smollett (in his much-cited 'Travels through France and Italy'), was prepared to admit that the coast in these parts was quite *'delightful'*, with its cover of *'green olives'* and with *'large trees of sweet myrtle growing wild'* aligning the main road along the shoreline from Cannes. But he said little of Antibes itself. In his view it was but *'a small maritime town, tolerably well fortified'*. A few years later, another British traveller, Arthur Young, blandly observed that *'Antibes, being a frontier town, is regularly fortified; the mole is pretty, and the view from it pleasing'*.

With the onset of the French Revolutionary Wars, Antibes was inevitably a major node of military activity, and very much a no-go area as far as any foreign visitors were concerned. The town's garrison was the base from which in 1792 General Anselme launched his thrust into the Kingdom of Piedmont-Sardinia. Two years later, as part of that military incursion, Bonaparte arrived in Antibes. On his way to Nice to take up his new position as artillery commander, he too must have been sufficiently taken with the place. So much so, that he saw fit to settle members of his family locally. With the Terror raging elsewhere in France, they set up residence in Château Salé, located just over a kilometre outside the town, and on the road to Grasse.

Antibes was to fare well during the Empire, and a number of its citizens reached positions of prominence, both within the military and within institutions of the State. But the years that immediately followed the restoration of the French monarchy saw little change in the economic and social life of the town. It continued to benefit from passing trade, but few improvements had been made *'intra muros'* to encourage those visiting from abroad to linger for any length of time. In a guidebook, published in 1847, Antibes was summarily described as *'a flourishing little sea-port'*. It then went on to suggest that if they were seeking to change horses there, then travellers should halt outside the gates and send in for them. In this way: *'They will save time, and their carriage will escape the risks of accidents, in being twice dragged through the most odious streets'*. Not the strongest of commendations.

However, a year or so later, and fully apprised of the dramatic changes taking place elsewhere along the coast, Jean Pierre Depigny, in a study of the town's historical development and future prospects, begged to differ. He argued that Antibes and its region had in fact much to interest the foreign visitor. Writing in 1849, he suggested that the main reason for its neglect was that:

> *'... nobody knows Antibes. The traveller has always passed by without entering (the town); without realizing that behind its menacing ramparts six thousand souls would receive him with kindness as long as he approaches them in a friendly manner. With its gentle climate, its pretty port, and its setting, which I have no fear in saying, is as beautiful as those of Naples and of Constantinople, (Antibes) has only one fault; that is to be located so far from Paris, and on a road that is so little frequented. Nowhere will one find more delicious fruits and a population that is better or prettier.*[1]

He continued, but in somewhat maudlin vein:

> *'Today, whoever is obliged to come to Antibes for personal reasons or on business, will start to feel sad two weeks before having to take his leave; his family will be in tears'.*

Despite Depigny's protestations, throughout the first half of the 19th century, the Antibes region remained very much a place to be bypassed, at least as far as most foreign visitors to the coast were concerned. All that was about to change, however, following its linkage with the national railway network. When the first trains started arriving at Antibes, following the opening of its station in 1862, the resident populace and local chambers of commerce no doubt thought that the locality was about to experience a dramatic transformation in its economic fortunes. It was hoped, in particular, that tourists and travellers would now stop off, and that some would choose to stay on, even if only for a short period during the winter season. It was important that they did, for, following the annexation of the County of Nice in 1860, the town's status as a military garrison was less secure; like a stranded vessel it had lost its strategic *raison d'être*. At this time Antibes and surrounding areas could only boast a population of some 7,000 and there was a distinct possibility that it might now even start to fall; such was its demographic profile. Something had to be done to address the matter.

Breaking the Mould

In the same way that foreign *'hivernants'* shunned the Old Town cores of numerous coastal settlements across the Riviera, for example Nice, Cannes, Menton and Hyères, so too they continued to see little that was appealing in Antibes *intra muros*. The streets remained narrow and cluttered, and hotel accommodation

Viel Antibes (Rue de la République)

Viel Antibes (Safranier)

continued to be both limited and of a standard far below that increasingly expected.

Although it was a vibrant market centre for the region, higher order services of the type demanded by relatively wealthy visitors were virtually non-existent. By and large, Antibes was still seen as a rather provincial coastal settlement, serving an essentially rural hinterland. Although facilities were somewhat limited, its port continued to play an important part in the economic life of the town. There were some small-scale domestic industries round and about, but in general there was not much of particular consequence. Furthermore, despite no longer being located at a national frontier, for the time being at least, there was still a strong military presence; a feature that was not to the liking of many. The prominence of gas works, petrol storage cylinders, and a hangar for tramways did not help matters either.

However, some visitors to the coast found the town and its immediate hinterland to be of more than passing interest – it was undoubtedly different from most other settlements along the coast, and offered a more vernacular and provincial experience. The ambiance and coastal scene were certainly sufficiently appealing to attract interest from artists, and would continue to do so for many years to come. Their work would undoubtedly help broadcast the attractions of the locality to a wider audience. As it happened, most of those who set up their easels in the area did so on Cap d'Antibes. Their seascapes, views of the town from amidst pine groves and rocky foreshores, would do much to advertise the scenic charm of the area. No doubt it also encouraged some to think not just of paying a fleeting visit to the cape, but also of establishing residences there.

One early and particularly celebrated artist was Ernest Meissonier. Renowned throughout France for his graphic and detailed paintings, he arrived with his family by train in June 1868. Presumably, one of the reasons he chose to stay in the area was because of its association with key stages in the life of his hero, Emperor Napoleon I – in particular, his earlier military years, and the drama of the flight from Elba and the start of the Hundred Days. Based in Paris, Meissonier had gained widespread public acclaim and professional recognition, mainly through his meticulously executed paintings of some of Napoleon's military campaigns. These included such works as *Friedland*, *Austerlitz before the Charge*, *Napoléon on Campaign in 1814*, and *Napoléon and his Staff*.

As it turned out, Meissonier's stay in Antibes proved to be not only pleasurable, but also highly productive in terms of the development of his art. Here he found painting in the open air to be revelatory. Equally significant was the scope that this afforded for exploring alternative approaches to his work; approaches which saw him abandoning, at least for a while, *'his traditional obsession with historical authenticity in favour of creating eye-catching visual effects by means of a few salient touches of the brush'*.[2] It has been suggested that in so doing he was perhaps mindful of emerging

Ernest Meissonier

stylistic trends: trends that were soon to result in the flowering of 'Impressionism' as an artistic movement. Overall, Meissonier was clearly delighted with his visit to this rather forgotten part of the coast. Of his experience, gazing out from positions on Cap d'Antibes, he was to write:

'It is delightful to sun oneself in the brilliant life of the South, instead of wandering about like gnomes in the fog. The view at Antibes is one of the fairest sights in nature. Looking at that shining sea, as beautiful and as inimitable in colour as the sky itself, one dreams one sees the ships of Ulysses floating on it. The lines of the mountains are certainly quite as pure as those of Greece'.

With 'Impressionism' firmly in mind, another artist of considerable standing who was equally captivated by Cap d'Antibes was Claude Monet. Following a first visit to the coast with Auguste Renoir in 1883, he returned a number of times over the coming years. Later, in 1888, he considered staying in Château de la Pinède in the settlement that would become Juan-les-Pins. But he swiftly changed his mind when he saw that one of his artist friends back in Paris – Henri Harpignies – was there with a noisy and deflecting set of acolytes: *'une maison à peintres'*, as he put it. Not only that, the cost of 12 francs a day was deemed to be too expensive by far. He swiftly decided to move on. At first the weather in the locality was execrable, but soon with more balmy days ahead he was up at around 5am and painting feverishly. Monet had intended to stay for 15 days but remained in the area for three months.

He frequently took up vantage points on the promontory, from where he looked out across the bay to the walled town of Antibes, or set himself the daunting task of capturing the changing moods and colours of the sea. Often twisted coastal pines framed his paintings. Monet was clearly more than captivated with the setting. It tested him and his palette to distraction. In a letter to a friend he wrote:

'Je peins la ville d'Antibes, une petite ville fortifiée, toute dorée par le soleil, se détachant sur de belles montagnes bleues et roses et la chaîne des Alpes éternellement couvertes de neige. C'est si clair, si pur de rose et de bleu que la moindre touche pas juste fait une tache de saleté'.

[*I am painting the town of Antibes, a small fortified town, made golden by the sun, standing out against the beautiful blue and pink mountains and the chain of Alps eternally covered in snow. It is so clear, such a pure pink and blue, that the slightest mistake with the brush leaves a dirty smudge.*]

More than anything it was the 'magical light' (*cette lumière féerique*) that fascinated and challenged him. In a letter to his friend, the sculptor, Auguste Rodin, he noted: *'je m'escrime et lutte avec le soleil. Et quel soleil ici ! Il faudrait peindre ici avec de l'or et des pierreries!'*.

[*I wrestle and struggle with the sun. And what sun here! Here one should paint with gold and precious stones.*]

Claude Monet

Henri Harpignies

Despite all the challenges, Monet succeeded in completing 39 canvases. Back in Paris his paintings would attract considerable acclaim.

Although the set-up in Château de la Pinède was not to his liking, Monet was pleased to renew acquaintance with Henri Harpignies (1819-1916) – a respected landscape painter of the Barbizon School. The pair would have had much to talk about.

Whilst they may not have had an immediate impact on the promotion of the Cap d'Antibes, the old town and what would become Juan-les-Pins, the depictions of other artists (e.g. Eugène Boudin, Alexander Werner, Vincent Courdouan, Ernest Buttura, Fausto Zonaro, Charles Labor, Emmanule Costa, Jean Monier de La Sizeranne) would most certainly also have helped in drawing the wider public's attention to the mesmeric attributes of the area.

So too would some of the writings of another of Monet's friends, Guy de Maupassant (see 2). Although he had first paid a visit to the coast in 1882, it was not until the winter of 1884/85 that Maupassant actually took up residence in the area. At this time, he based himself in Cannes. On his next visit, however, just before Xmas 1885, he rented a Provençal villa, located not far beyond the ramparts of Antibes, and on the edge of Cap d'Antibes. It was here in Villa Bosquet that he worked on his novel *Mont-Oriol*. Also resident were Maupassant's mother and his dutiful servant – François Tassart. When not entrenched in his study, he was often to be seen either walking through the olive groves and moorland tracts on the cape or, more often than not, on board his yacht

'Louisette', which he berthed nearby in the small harbour then known as Port Aubernon. For the seven months, October 1886 to April 1887, the Maupassants moved to another residence – *Chalet des Alpes*, located on the hill slopes of the Badine district, just to the west of Antibes. Maupassant clearly felt at home in the area. Thus, in his short story, *Madame Parisse*, a character notes:

> '*I was sitting on the pier of the small port of Obernon (sic), near the village of Salis, looking at Antibes, bathed in the setting sun. I had never before seen anything so wonderful and so beautiful*'.

But not everyone was so sanguine as to the town's longer-term prospects. Thus, in a text published in 1885, for instance, Charlotte Dempster[3] expressed her personal view that Antibes was '*a dull, sleepy little place where everything is on a miniature scale – the port, the garrison, the mole, the esplanade and the old citadel...*' She then asserts that whilst access to fresh water via an ancient aqueduct was a major positive feature, not so the town itself. Thus, as others had earlier pronounced, she opined that '*the streets are so narrow that to drive a pair of horses through them is a trial to the nerves...*'. Whilst this may have been the case, it was hardly a devastating critique. On a much more positive note, however, she was prepared to proclaim that: '*There is no part of Provence that is fairer than this promontory of Antibes*. By promontory, she was presumably referring to Cap d'Antibes.

In his seminal text, Stéphen Liégeard also expressed his concern as to the future of the town and its populace. Whilst admitting that Antibes was still worthy of a visit, he was also of the firm opinion that if the local authorities wished to take full advantage of the opportunities that existed, particularly in regard to the promotion of tourism and residential development, then a necessary first step would be to secure its formal 'declassification' as a military garrison. As it happened, the necessary submissions to central government had already been effected as far back as 1872. Not only that, in 1877 a further application by the municipal authority requested control over the open ground surrounding the fortifications (*zones de servitudes*). Covering some 25 hectares this zone had long been a no-go military area; now, if given the necessary permission, it too could open new possibilities for development. But with legal and

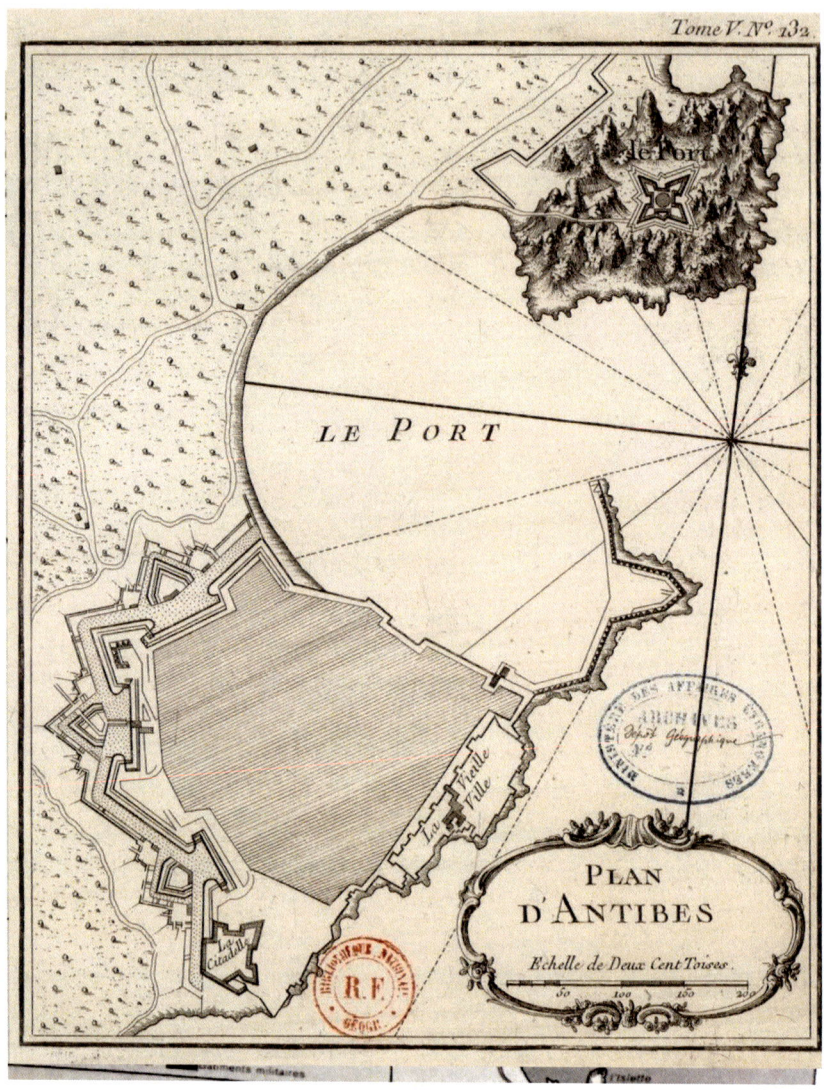

Old Town and Line of Fortifications
Gallica.bnf.fr

bureaucratic processes being what they were, the full package of formal declassification was only secured by convention in 1895. Hopefully, the town was now ready to forge ahead. The first step would be to dismantle a large section of the walls, bastions and ramparts.

As it turned out, this task proved to be more onerous and costly than had been expected. It soon became clear that the local authority would need outside help. Thus it was that the services of an experienced developer – Ernest Macé – had to be called upon to direct the programme of works. As far as the internal restructuring of the town was concerned, an important prerequisite was ensuring that certain key spaces were kept in the public domain. Included among them were Place Nationale and Cours Masséna. They had long been areas of vibrant public concourse and of sundry commercial activities. But a *sine qua non* was that barracks and associated military paraphernalia were moved out of the centre of the town, thereby helping to soften the image and overall feel of the place. Not only that, new development opportunities would hopefully open up.

One of the first schemes of work involved the removal/ restructuring of certain of the main gates (*poternes*) – in particular Porte Royale and Porte Sainte-Claire. The latter would certainly facilitate smoother access to Cap d'Antibes. But then the gargantuan task of removing the walls and facing the disruption that would inevitably ensue had to be faced by the local populace. However, in the eyes of many it was all worth it. Antibes could now look forward to making the transition from being a '*place de guerre*' and become '*une ville de saison*'.

But all this would come at a price. Conscious of alternative arguments, especially in regard to the loss of heritage, Liégeard was at pains to stress that, despite the proposed destruction of the fortifications, the town itself still had much of historical and architectural interest, even for the most casual and uninitiated of visitors. At the very least it was still quaint and very different. In a final flourish, he proclaimed that the *'Vieille Ville'* was, and would remain, *'coquettishly respectable'* – whatever that might mean!

With declassification finally secured, it was expected that the heavy work of dismantling the fortifications would be accomplished within six years. This would turn out to be wishful thinking, for the whole exercise proved to be a slow, taxing and costly undertaking. But at the very least much of the stone and rubble could now be used as infill on neighbouring coastal flats, creating yet more space for recreational areas, promenades, housing and hotels. In so doing, it would also ensure a more attractive and seamless link with Cap d'Antibes.

While most locals were seemingly delighted with the project, some continued to balk at the prospect of a much-reduced role for the garrison. Others, however, were more concerned that dismantlement (*dérasement*) of the ramparts on the landward side of the town would rob it not only of its unique character, but also destroy a prized cultural asset. There was nowhere like it, they claimed, across the whole length of the Côte d'Azur.

Three notable personages who were more than displeased with what they regarded as a sorry disfiguration were Guy de Maupassant himself, together with the writer, political activist and arch-feminist, Juliette Adam. She had a villa nearby in Golfe-Juan. Also voicing his considerable displeasure was the Provençal poet and writer, Paul Arène. In Antibes he was held in particularly high esteem.

As it turned out, some sections of the ramparts, on the seaward side and around the harbour, were left untouched. Fort Carré was such a monolithic and stunning feature that it too escaped demolition. But over large sections the process of clearance still went ahead.

Interestingly, a number of foreign visitors to the town also expressed their dismay at what was happening. Thus, in 1907, William Scott[4] considered it to be pure vandalism. Clearly overwhelmed at what was happening, his diatribe is worth quoting in full. Of Antibes, he stated:

Antibes, Juan-les-Pins and Cap d'Antibes

Antibes: Coastal Ramparts

'Its inhabitants would probably resent the implied suggestion, but those who knew and loved the old city a quarter of a century ago, and now come back to its site in the hope of renewing their acquaintance and old associations, will stand horror-struck and aghast at the spectacle. Nearly everything which was of value has disappeared. Antibes is no more. It was formerly one of the specimens, yearly becoming rarer, of walled towns with their ramparts intact, the very breath of the Middle Ages exhaling from their stones. Its past stretched away to the mists of antiquity, when it was founded by early Greek settlers. Its history has been from time immemorial bound up with the vicissitudes of our Riviera. Its "battles, sieges, fortunes" had endeared it worthy of respect; and yet everything has been wantonly, needlessly, and uselessly sacrificed to a pestilent craze for modernity, and the mad fury of a conscienceless passion for speculation. If ever the destruction of ancient landmarks deserved reprobation, if ever the spoiler's hand merited unsparing blame, it is in the case of the

destruction of Antibes. Not one single valid argument can be adduced, not one single pretension made good, to justify the wilful, conscious, and relentless ruin which has wrought havoc with this splendid record of the past. In a public square of the present town is a monument which the inhabitants have erected in memory – if you please – of their own valour! They should now proceed to erect by its side another monument to commemorate their unutterable and insensate folly. Posterity will no doubt do it for them, and in no unhesitating terms, but nothing can bring back the lost links with the past, the perished treasures of antiquity that passed away when the speculator's pickaxe levelled down the age-stained walls of old Antibes'.

Equally damning was the writer Loveland. He proclaimed that 'the disappearance of the beautiful old ramparts had destroyed all of the picturesqueness (sic) of the town, which today is an open, windy, ugly place, in an awkward stage of development so frequently to be met with in British seaside resorts'.

In marked contrast, however, the noted travel writer, Augustus Hare, visited Antibes in 1896, just as the work to remove the town walls was getting under way. Strangely, he made no mention of such matters in his guide to the area. For it was clearly not seen to be an issue. Overall, Hare would appear to have been singularly impressed with the town and its setting. Thus, he wrote:

'The town, as seen from a little creek beyond the fort, with its bastions and lofty orange-coloured towers, juts out most picturesquely into the sea, and has a background of marvellous beauty in the long range of peaks of the Maritime Alps, always white with snow in winter. Indeed, those who linger to enjoy this scene from one of the coves of the western bay, in the orange lights and pink shadows of sunset, will agree that it is the most beautiful seaside view in France'.[5]

Whatever the differing stances on the matter, with the removal of large landward sections of its walls eventually completed, the town council was now in a position to embark on the task of

Antibes, Juan-les-Pins and Cap d'Antibes

Antibes

fashioning a whole new suburban area, one in which wealthy foreigners and property developers in particular would see fit to invest. Now, the way was cleared for a steady encroachment onto the in-filled grounds that stretched out towards Cap d'Antibes and the woodlands that draped the flanks of the Plateau de la Garoupe (see 2). The area that had once been rough, open terrain and that had formed part of the garrison's defensive system would soon be criss-crossed by a lattice of wide new roads. Tree-lined boulevards were laid out (e.g. Boulevard Albert 1er, Boulevard Maréchal Foche, Avenue Robert Soleau), and a substantial town square (Place Macé, now Place de Gaulle) was established near the former main gate of the town. Around the square, residences, shops and the imposing Grand Hôtel also became notable features.

In no time, close to the foreshore, hotels and pensions, would be welcoming long-awaited guests. Along the length of the main boulevards, building plots (*lotissements*) were also made available

Place Macé (now Charles de Gaulle) and the Grand Hôtel

Boulevard Albert Premier

Le Port d'Antibes (Port Vauban)

for the construction of private residences (*pavillons*) in varying architectural styles, including Art Deco. Slowly, fashionable shops also grew in number. Together, all these initiatives freshened up the overall ambiance. Also proving to be particularly significant was the construction in 1919 of the wide thoroughfare, later to be named Boulevard Wilson, it was to become a key linkage with the resort of Juan-le-Pins. The coastal road hugging parts of the rocky shoreline of the cape was steadily extended and upgraded. The port too was improved and became increasingly busy.

For the town and the immediate locality the economic future was soon looking that much brighter. But there were still those, fewer in number, who remained unconvinced, and continued to be disenchanted with the wave of new developments.

The Making of Juan-les-Pins

In the opening entry to his quasi-diary (*Sur l'eau*), dated April 1884, Guy de Maupassant describes sailing his yacht '*Bel Ami*' into the

Baie de Golfe Juan, after having rounded Cap d'Antibes (see 2). In so doing he looked out on the coastline before him and, among other observations, suggested that the littoral would soon be attracting visitors in considerable numbers. All that was now needed was for shrewd developers or syndicates to come along. As it happened, at the time that he was musing on such matters, moves in that direction were already underway, and had been for a number of years. For in 1881 an investment company, named the *'Société Foncière de Cannes et du Littoral'* (SFCL) had been established by the *'La Banque Antoine Rigal de Cannes'*, and was already in the process of buying up tracts of land and dividing them up into lots ready for the construction of villas and hotels. From the outset, the investment company focused in particular on a then small coastal hamlet located on the edge of Cap d'Antibes, and just a mile or two across the neck of land that separated it from the town of Antibes. At the time, the location concerned comprised just a few residences, cabins and beach structures. Services and other facilities of any consequence were few in number. A distinctive and defining feature of the area were clumps of pines that offered fragrant shelter. They

La Pinède and Early Villas

would later figure in the naming of the nascent settlement.

As far as the SFCL itself was concerned, it had been fortunate in securing the patronage of an exalted shareholder – Leopold, Duke of Albany, the youngest son of Queen Victoria. Such was his status that serious consideration was given to naming the new settlement *Albany-les-Pins*. That proposal was not, however, to be followed through. It would have been untimely if it had been, for in 1884 Leopold, who suffered from haemophilia, died following complications from a fall while staying in Cannes. He was just 31 years of age. Needless to say, his passing deprived the company both of a name and a royal figurehead who would undoubtedly have helped, as Liégeard put it, to lure potential investors of some substance (*'appâter le chaland'*). Regarding the settlement's name, suggested alternatives, such as Heliopolis and Antibes-les-Pins, were eventually rejected in favour of Juan-les-Pins. It was the mayor of Antibes at the time, Monsieur Vial, who apparently proposed the new designation. This was in 1882. After much lobbying, the whole venture was given a much-needed boost with the opening in 1884 of a dedicated station on the PLM railway line that ran along the coastal fringe and linked the emerging resort to Cannes and Nice and places beyond.

As it was to turn out, the development company soon encountered financial difficulties and was eventually wound up. But with other promoters waiting eagerly in the wings, the construction programme regained momentum. One of the first major hotels to be established was Hôtel de la Réserve. Opened in 1891, among its early guests was Guy de Maupassant himself. A few years later, the nascent resort received a major boost following the inauguration in 1894 of the Grand Hôtel de Juan-les-Pins. Boasting a range of modern amenities, including hot water, central heating and electricity no less, it had 60 rooms and a garden that stretched down to the sea, and most important of all, access to a fine sandy beach. The hotel may not have matched the monumental palaces of Nice and Cannes, but it would most certainly have helped to put Juan-les-Pins more firmly on the map. Whilst the Grand Hôtel loomed large, throughout the locality the construction of new villas, together with more modest hotels and guesthouses to suit all tastes and pockets, gathered pace. The opening of a municipal casino on the foreshore in 1909, following supportive national legislation concerning such establishments, helped to further affirm the resort's status as a formally classified 'station balnéaire'.

But then came the Great War. As elsewhere along the coast, all plans for the burgeoning resort had to be put on hold. There may not have been many tourists about, but the growing number of military personnel, especially Americans, who had been sent south to convalesce, often made their way to Juan. There, they took full advantage of the opportunity to rest up for a while on nearby beaches, bask in the sunshine and to swim in warm waters. Significantly, they often did so during the months of summer. In so doing, at least according to some commentators, they were the ones who unwittingly initiated a vogue of considerable consequence for resorts throughout the Riviera.

Some, however, have offered alternative explanations as to how it all came about (see below), but there is no doubting that Juan-les-Pins soon found itself at the epicentre of a cultural transformation that would sweep through resorts across the Riviera. Since the middle part of the nineteenth century, they had been overwhelmingly dependent on welcoming the vast majority of visitors during the winter period. Now it was the months of summer that would come to the fore. It was a slowish process at first, but the transformation would steadily gain momentum, and eventually come to dominate. Not that the old guard suddenly disappeared. For some time to come they would continue to settle in for the traditional winter season. The hospitality sector at large could now look forward to receiving visitors throughout the year.

In seeking to explain the emergence of the summer season, many writers have focussed in particular on the supposedly formative role played in the early 1920s by a chance set of encounters that

Juan-les-Pins

Entre CANNES et NICE (Alpes-Maritimes)

Station du P.-L.-M., une demi-heure de Nice

Située à égale distance de Nice et de Cannes, la station de **Juan-les-Pins** offre, avec de précieux avantages climatériques, la plus belle plage du littoral méditerranéen, au fond du golfe Juan. Complètement abrité des vents du nord, d'un climat délicieusement tempéré, **Juan-les-Pins**, est à la fois station d'hiver et d'été; comme centre d'excursions, il est admirablement placé et peut servir de point de départ aux innombrables

LE GRAND HOTEL OUVERT TOUTE L'ANNÉE

promenades dans les régions si pittoresques du *cap d'Antibes*, de *Grasse*, de *Cannes* et de *l'Estérel*.

Le Grand Hôtel de Juan-les-Pins (H. Lubcké, Directeur-Propriétaire), est un établissement de premier ordre, installé avec tout le confort moderne, au milieu d'un grand jardin anglais planté de mimosas et de plantes exotiques, dominant la mer en plein midi, à proximité des forêts de pins et qui offre toutes les ressources pour des séjours prolongés. Un établissement de bains, *Calypso*, inauguré en 1902, dépendant de l'hôtel, comprend un restaurant, un café, une salle de fêtes, des salons particuliers, des cabines et une terrasse sur la superbe plage de sable fin, où l'on peut aller à plus de 60 mètres dans la mer sans perdre pied.

took place, just a short distance away from Juan on Cap d'Antibes. Whether or not those involved could be considered as the prime movers in the promotion of a summer season is debatable. What *is* certain, however, is that the small group of individuals concerned were certainly highly influential in stimulating interest in the area; for at the time they happened to be key figures in the worlds of literature, painting, dance and music.

The Lost Generation Arrive

The story, as often told, begins with the chance decision taken by Cole Porter, the acclaimed American singer and lyricist, together with his new wife, Linda Lee Thomas, to take their leave of Paris and to make their way south to the Riviera. They were on their honeymoon. It was high summer in 1921 when they arrived. Much to their surprise, they discovered that all was quiet. Major hotels and other facilities were shut down, or operating at very much reduced levels. Presumably, the Porters were not fully aware of this when they arrived, or it was of no particular consequence to them. They were happy just driving and ambling around, exploring the region and settling in where they could. At one point, and seemingly by chance, the newly-weds found themselves on Cap d'Antibes.

Cole and Linda were clearly impressed with the locality. Calm, with small beaches and all-embracing sea-views, they took the decision to linger a while and to seek out a befitting place to stay. With Linda being a so-called 'alimony million heiress', and Cole being of no small means, they could well afford to rent a substantial property. Thus it was that they chanced upon Château de la Garoupe.[6] It was available for a short let and more than fitted the bill. Located not far from Villa Eilenroc and Grand Hôtel du Cap (see 2 and 3), it belonged to a British family, the McLarens/Normans (see 5). Noted for its secluded location amidst pinewoods, the stunning outlook from its terrace, the central pathway stretching down to a sheltered cove, together with the well-tended gardens, it was an ideal retreat for a romantic *'lune de miel'*. Clearly enchanted, the couple decided to settle in for what, we must assume, was an intimate two-week stay. Château de la Garoupe and the ambiance clearly left its mark, for the following year the couple booked in again for another summer stay. Cole was soon informing his friends back in Paris, and elsewhere, of the exceptional charm of the locality. He would later recall:

> 'we rented the Château de la Garoupe for two summers – 1921 and 1922 – and enjoyed every moment. But in those days we were considered crazy and it was before the days anyone went to the Riviera in the summer, as the weather was considered too hot.'

Significantly, during their second visit the Porters invited two scions of exceedingly wealthy American families to join them – the couple Gerald and Sara Murphy, together with their three children. Gerald and Cole had known each other at Yale, and had renewed their acquaintanceship in Paris where, at that time, so many Americans were gathered, mainly seeking an escape from Prohibition and bourgeois mores back home. Needless to say, the considerable strength of the dollar also helped. Everything seemed so cheap – living was easy. Paris for the Murphys was: *'alluring, polymorphous and perverse'*, for there was a *'tension and excitement in the air that was almost physical'*.

Seduced by the cultural life of the city, Gerald took the decision to abandon his humdrum plans to establish himself as a landscape architect. He now dreamt of metamorphosing into an accomplished painter. In this, and guided in particular by the Russian artist, Natalia Goncharova, he was surprisingly successful; to the extent that within a relatively short space of time he would be exhibiting acknowledged works in the *Salon des Indépendants*. While in Paris, the Murphys socialised and collaborated with a wide array of personalities, celebrated (or soon to be celebrated) in their particular cultural fields. They included, among many others: Pablo Picasso, Fernand Léger, Jean Cocteau, Serge Diaghilev, Igor

Stravinsky, Ernest Hemingway, F. Scott Fitzgerald, Miro, Ezra Pound, and Gertrude Stein. Gerald also found working for the *Ballets Russes* to be particularly stimulating.

For the Murphys, meeting up with the Porters on Cap d'Antibes in 1923 would also turn out to be a life-changing experience. So taken were they with the area that they decided to set up a home for themselves nearby. Whilst searching around for a suitable property, and themselves needing a temporary place to stay, the Murphys managed to persuade the circumspect owner of the Hôtel du Cap, Antoine Sella, to keep his hotel open for a few months. As already noted, normally, like most other grand hotels on the Côte d'Azur, it was closed down and mothballed between May and September. There was little point in staying open during the summer months since the traditional clientele were off indulging themselves elsewhere in cooler parts of Europe – mountain spas and the coastal resorts of Normandy, for example.

Sella initially demurred. But on further reflection, however, he relented, agreeing to open up merely the ground floor of the establishment. What was there to lose? After all this was at a time when he had just completed the celebrated extension to the main hotel – Pavillon Eden Roc (see 3). Little did Sella realize it, but in keeping his hotel open for business on this particular occasion (albeit only partially so), he was taking a tentative step towards a future year-round opening of his hotel; and that, reputedly, at the behest of a persuasive American, he would be helping to further a trend that other hoteliers would soon be emulating. That Sella was hesitant at the time is surprising since he would have known that as far back as 1895, publicity notices for the nearby Grand Hôtel de Juan-les-Pins highlighted the fact that the establishment was open all the year round.

It not necessary to take such matters further, apart from noting that it was also at around the time that the Murphys were staying there, Sella thought he could relax traditional protocol by inviting the bevy of young ladies attending the Margaret Morris Summer

School nearby (see 3). As will be elaborated upon later, the ladies concerned caught the penetrating eye of Pablo Picasso who had been invited to meet up with the Murphys at the hotel for a part of their summer sojourn. Picasso turned up in August together with his Ukrainian wife Olga (née Khokhlova), their young son Paulo, and Picasso's mother, Dona Maria.[7]

As it happened, Picasso and Olga were no strangers to Cap d'Antibes. Indeed as recently as 1918, and during high summer no less, they had rented a villa located just outside of Juan-les-Pins. Olga was pregnant at the time, and for the couple it proved to be a memorable stay, one in which they bonded well. As Picasso's biographer, John Richardson would later claim: *'Pregnancy and the blazing southern sun melted Olga's northern formality'*.[8] For Picasso it also turned out to be a highly productive time in terms of his own work. *'The atavistic pull of the Mediterranean'*[9] had apparently worked its magic. But for Olga it was to be a short-lived idyllic escape, well away from the strains that life in Paris would later place on their relationship.[10]

As to the Murphys and their search for a more permanent base on Cap d'Antibes, they eventually found just the sort of property

Picasso and Olga Khokhlova

they had been looking for. Rather unimaginatively, it was to be named Villa America. Over the coming years the couple would throw themselves whole-heartedly into rebuilding, renovating and refurbishing what was a relatively modest villa. With a beguiling and aromatic tropical garden to set the place off, the couple would soon be inviting guests down for the summer. They were long known to be generous hosts. Of those arriving from Paris, a number had close links with the Ballets Russes. They may not have met up, but it is certain that in times past, members of the Romanov family, who were now living within a stone's throw of Villa America, would have at least known of the Russian dancers and choreographers currently working for Diaghilev's company. How times and circumstances had changed for all concerned.

Later, reminiscing on the heady days spent on Cap d'Antibes and Cole Porter's role in drawing attention to the area, Gerald would write:

> 'Cole always had great originality about finding new places and at that time no one ever went near the Riviera in summer. The English and the Germans – there were no longer any Russians – who came down for the short spring season closed their villas as soon as it began to get warm. None of them ever went into the water, you see. When we went to visit Cole, it was hot, hot summer, but the air was dry, and it was cool in the evening, and the water was that wonderful jade-and-amethyst color (sic). Right out on the end of the Cap there was a tiny beach – the Garoupe – only about forty yards long and covered with a bed of sea-weed (sic) that must have been four feet thick. We dug out a corner of the beach and bathed there and sat in the sun, and we decided this is where we wanted to be. Oddly, Cole never came back'.

His remark concerning Russians is a little strange, for apart from the Romanovs who would later be living nearby, and of whose presence he must certainly have been aware, Gerald was bound to have known of the plight of the many exiles then struggling to make ends meet in resorts across the Riviera. Indeed among the domestic staff appointed to help look after Villa America and, in his particular case, to serve also as a tutor to the couple's children, was an aristocratic Russian exile – Vladimir Orloff. The Murphys had first met him in Paris, when he was working with Diaghilev's company as a painter of backdrops and stage sets for ballet productions. He too had managed to flee his homeland, but his titled father would not do so, having been executed by the Bolsheviks. Vladimir became a trusted member of the family. Later on, his skilled interest in boat design proved to be especially useful and he was ultimately responsible for the construction and servicing of several sea-going craft used by the family. Whether or not he joined any of the organisations, set up by Russian exiles living on the Côte d'Azur, has not been reported, nor whether there were any chance encounters with the Romanovs then resident in the vicinity.

The Murphys quickly established a routine in Villa America. Mornings for Gerald meant working in his studio; for Sara it was a question of managing the house and garden, and ensuring that their children were suitably educated. Shortly before noon the whole clan, plus honoured guests, would, weather permitting, move down onto the nearby beach at La Garoupe. There, having cleared swathes of the aforementioned seaweed, games, physical exercises and other entertainments were duly organized. Sherry would be taken as an aperitif before

Gerald and Sara Murphy, Plage de la Garoupe, Cap d'Antibes

lunch was served back at the villa on the embowered terrace. Siestas, more games for the children, or trips out into old Antibes and the surrounding countryside would account for the remaining part of the afternoon. In the evening everyone was expected to dress for dinner – on the terrace *'under the linden tree the women in their beaded dresses and the men in their dinner jackets, with everyone so young and merry and clever'*.[11]

Reminiscing, the novelist and playwright friend, Donald Ogden Stewart, remarked of the Murphys that: *'they had the gift of making life enchantingly pleasurable for those who were fortunate enough to be their friends'*. But not all those taking advantage of their conviviality and largesse would respond befittingly at all times. This was most certainly the case as far as two freewheeling American arrivals were concerned – Scott and Zelda Fitzgerald. By then Scott had published his first two novels – *This Side of Paradise* (1920) and *The Beautiful and the Damned* (1922). The following year *The Great Gatsby*, which many have considered to be a translocation of Riviera society to Long Island, New York, would be greeted with considerable acclaim.

Escaping from America in a vain attempt to lead a quieter social life, the Fitzgeralds had first settled in Paris (where they met the Murphys), but had then quickly retreated south to the Riviera coastal town of St Raphael. It was from there that they travelled over to Cap d'Antibes. Impressed, they soon chose to base themselves nearby in Juan-les-Pins. There they rented Villa Saint Louis, which would later become a noted hotel, as indeed it still is.[12] For the Fitzgeralds their stay was often traumatic, with Zelda seemingly on a pathway to self-destruction. For the couple, reckless, drink-fuelled behaviour was all too often par for the course, and embarrassingly so for all those who happened to be in their company. But somehow the Murphys, ever sympathetic and accommodating, managed to cope when in their unsettling company. The time that the Fitzgeralds spent with the Murphys on Cap d'Antibes may have often been manic, but at least it supplied

Scott with templates for the two main characters in a later novel – Dick and Nicole Diver in *Tender is the Night*. It was published in 1934 and carried an apposite dedication: to *'Gerald and Sara – many fêtes'*. In the novel, it is asked whether the Divers had liked life on the French Riviera; the telling response was: *'They have to, they invented it.'*

As if the Fitzgeralds were not enough, in 1925 Ernest Hemingway and his wife, Hadley, arrived to join the party. The Hemingways also chose to stay in Juan-les-Pins where they rented Villa Paquita. By then Juan was the in-place to be. In his memoirs, published in 1964, three years after his death, and subsequently entitled *A Moveable Feast*, Hemingway recalled, in inimitable style:

'Scott told me about the Riviera and how my wife and I must come there the next summer and how we would go there and how he would find a place for us that was not expensive and we would both work hard every day and swim and lie on the beach and be brown and only have a single aperitif before lunch and one before dinner. Zelda would be happy there, he said. She loved to swim and was a beautiful diver and she was happy with that life and would want him to work and everything would be disciplined. He and Zelda and their daughter were going to go there that summer'.

He also claimed that Scott had hoped that on the Riviera, away from the social distractions of Paris, he might be able to re-engage with his literary muse and find some much-needed solace. To some extent he did, but as Hemingway also recollected, all was not well with the Fitzgeralds:

'Scott and Zelda had been at Cap d'Antibes, and that fall when I saw him in Paris he was very changed. He had not done any sobering up on the Riviera and he was drunk now in the day-time (sic) as well as nights'.

In 1925 another high profile, but slightly less bibulous, American couple paying a visit to the Murphys were Frank Jay Gould and his third wife, Florence (née Lacaze).[13] Son, and legatee, of the immensely wealthy railway magnate Jay Gould, and a flourishing businessman in his own right, with lucrative investments in the rail and power generation sectors, Frank Jay had left America in 1913, and like ever-increasing numbers of his compatriots, sought to explore pastures new in France. At the time he was still married to his second wife, Edith Kelly, and it was not until 1919 that he secured the longed-for divorce. It was while indulging himself in the miscellany of delights that Paris had to offer, that he would succumb to the charms of Florence, an American of French parentage.

Florence Lacaze knew exactly what she wanted out of life and, after a failed first marriage, set about achieving it in single-minded fashion. Although she harboured ambitions as a professional opera singer, for her, money, power and status, were of the utmost importance. So too was having fun. Realising that all this was not to be had back home, she too had headed for Paris. It was there in her late 20s that Florence succeeded in establishing a relationship with Frank. He was just the sort of wealthy man-about-town she was looking for. With guile, she snared her prey. Frank was 46 when in 1923 they were married. From the outset both parties agreed that, on the conjugal front at least, it was to be a relaxed and open arrangement; but that when it came to business matters they would operate as a tightly knit and single-minded team. Within no time at all the couple would immerse themselves with verve in the ever-growing expatriate community. Florence was now in a position to hone her social skills and become yet another accomplished 'salonnière' within the Parisian 'beau monde', who were by now descending on the 'City of Light' in ever-increasing numbers.

Shortly after their marriage, and like the Porters just a year before them, the newly-weds headed south to the Riviera. They duly set up a base for themselves in Cannes, where they purchased a substantial residence.[14] As it turned out, they soon discovered that the enterprises in which they thought they might become fruitfully engaged, such as casinos and hotels, were, at least in that particular resort, more than amply catered for, and that there would be little point in seeking to enter the market. Accordingly, after a short stay in the area they returned to Paris to rethink the situation.

But the couple did not give up on their plans. They intended to return, and perhaps a little sooner than they had expected. With Frank not in the best of health, and needing to recuperate following a serious abdominal operation, the Côte d'Azur once again beckoned. What better place to relax and recover, whilst once again keeping a watchful eye out for possible business opportunities. Rather than settle in Cannes, the Goulds made their way to Cap d'Antibes and booked into the Grand Hôtel du Cap. They arrived in late September 1925 at the start of the traditional winter season. While there, living in the lap of luxury, they would no doubt have heard more from Antoine Sella of his first tentative steps towards a more regular opening up of his establishment during the months of summer. The Goulds would also have learnt more from the Murphys who, by now, were heavily involved in renovating Villa America nearby. At the same time they would have most certainly been apprised of the growing popularity of Juan-les-Pins as a playground for a new social set; in particular, a much younger and more boisterous crowd than had traditionally sojourned on the Côte d'Azur. The Goulds quickly sensed an emerging niche in the market; one that they could usefully exploit. Not only that, from what they had heard, Juan also seemed to be just the sort of place where they could, given a little time, become prime movers and shakers – cocks of the walk no less. It was a prospect that certainly appealed to Florence. The less ebullient Frank was simply looking forward to cutting deals behind the scenes and to cultivating local business and political links. He knew the name of the game.

Convinced that they had found a place where they could lead a full and enterprising life, the Goulds purchased another residence, the neo-Gothic 'Villa Vigie'. A singular feature of the property was that it had its own private beach, looking out over the Baie de Golf-Juan. For a short while at least, a less attractive feature was that renting accommodation very close-by were the Fitzgeralds. They were based in Villa St Louis. At the time, Scott was busy re-working his novel *The Great Gatsby*, whilst Zelda was taking every opportunity to let her hair down, much to the embarrassment on occasions of the Murphys. Florence Gould enjoyed Zelda's manic exuberance at first, but it would eventually become too much of an embarrassment. With Frank looking disapprovingly on, their relationship cooled. Also hovering around were the Hemingways – Ernest, his first wife Hadley (Richardson) and their child Jack. By then their marriage was doomed, and divorce soon followed in 1927.

Frank Gould made his first bold move into the property and hospitality market in Juan by joining forces with an experienced restaurateur – Edouard Baudoin. In 1923 Baudoin had purchased the local casino. It had seen better days and was in need of a significant upgrade. Within no time, the 'Casino de Juan-les-Pins'

Casino Entrance

was welcoming a steady flow of eager punters through its doors.

Frank and Edouard's first fully joint venture was monumental. It involved the construction of a vast and luxurious hotel that was to be called 'Hôtel Provençal'. Designed by Lucien Sable, an architect based in Cannes, in style it merged Art Deco and neo-Provençal elements. With Frank's local contacts suitably primed, planning permissions were secured in extra quick time and, amazingly, the hotel opened its doors in 1927. It added a striking note of upmarket elegance to the resort, which until then had remained rather low-key in its ambitions, focusing on a more youthful and exuberant, but still monied, clientele. Set back, but a small distance from the seashore and fronted by a grove of palms, 'Hôtel Provençal' was to have over 250 swish apartments. The complex included modern bars, gaming rooms and restaurants in variety. With landscaped gardens enclosing the structure, and with facilities available on site for sundry physical and recreational activities, it catered for all modern tastes. Reputedly, Antoine Sella in the Grand Hôtel du

Frank Jay Gould

Florence Gould

Le Provençal

Cap was less than pleased with the intensity of the competition that this new entrant in the local hotel sector might pose, but he need not have worried, it only encouraged him to up his stakes.

Meanwhile, with visitor numbers gathering pace, the Goulds also invested in two existing hotels – Hôtel Alba and Hôtel des Deux Plages – and set about their refurbishment. Inevitably, other investors in hotels would eventually arrive on the scene. Interestingly, two hotels that would steadily gain reputations for themselves were owned and managed by Russian exiles. In 1927 a young Russian Jew, named Boma Estène, leased the very villa that a few years earlier had been rented out to the Fitzgeralds – Villa Saint Louis, and began the process of steadily turning it into a modest guesthouse. Together with his wife, Simone – daughter of a local hotelier family – he gradually extended and refreshed the property. Ideally situated on the seafront, in 1929 the boutique hotel opened its doors, under the banner Hôtel Belles Rives.[15] Not far away, in 1931 another Russian – Alexandre Barache – opened a popular Art Deco themed hotel – Hôtel Juana.[16]

Also taking advantage of new opportunities it was inevitable that new restaurants, nightclubs, bars and other social venues would emerge. Some of the most frequented were Maxim's, the Hôtel Pin Doré, La Cage au Poule and Le Pré Catalan. With all that was going on, it was little wonder that the resort would soon be referred to

Hôtel Pin Doré

by some as *'Juan Canaille'* – 'vulgar', a place where riff-raff and the 'lesser world of frivolity' gathered.

But for the growing number of visitors it was a go-to place, especially for those looking for a more laid-back and fun-loving holiday experience. After the austerities and ravages of war it was time for a change. This would manifest itself in numerous ways, but perhaps most felicitously in fashion. As far as young women in particular were concerned, no longer would the heavy, dark, down to the ankles garb of yesteryear be deemed suitable attire. Former straitlaced taboos had to be jettisoned, so that the physical side of life could be fully disported and exercised. The release from fusty, all-encompassing and corseted dress was revolutionary. For those now descending on the area, lighter attire, plunging necklines, all suitably adorned with modern, showy accessories (strings of beads being a notable feature) became the order of the day, and of the night. The process of emancipation, for that is what it was, further manifested itself in hairstyles. The fashion now was for boyishly bobbed crops. Where deemed appropriate, they were suitably topped with floppy broad-brimmed hats. Inevitably, fashion houses responded quickly to the craze for lively and daring experimentation in dress. Thus it was, apparently following a proposal from Florence Gould, that her friend Gabrielle 'Coco' Chanel came up with the concept of beach pyjamas. Soon they too were all the rage. So much so, that in the press, Juan was being referred to as 'Pyjamapolis'. Light, low cut and colourful, and often sporting Art-Deco designs, they were suitably provocative for the times. Loose fitting and fresh, they, along with other avant-garde styles, were ideal for promenading during hot summer days, and equally suitable for night-time revelries. They most certainly chimed with the wilder dance crazes then in vogue – the Charleston, the Black Bottom, to cite but two. Blues and jazz soon pervaded the hot, perfumed and sensual air. Maxime's in particular was an especially popular venue.

Whilst such changes in women's fashion grabbed the headlines, menswear also experienced shifts in style, although less markedly so. Looser trousers were a feature, but it was perhaps in beach and sports attire that such trends were most on display.

Accompanying these developments, and one that would prove to be a significant cultural shift was a transformation in attitudes towards the sun and sunbathing. Whereas in the past those of high society who made their way down to the shores of the Mediterranean (albeit in the winter period) made a conscious effort to shield their bodies from the darkening

Promenade in Juan-les-Pins.

effects of sunlight on the skin, now such exposure was in vogue. Reputedly, it was Chanel again who set the movement in motion. It was to be yet another radical development. Bronzing was now *à la mode*. The body was to be openly displayed, and hopefully admired. In that sense, it was part of a wider on-going sexual revolution.

Allied with all this was an increasing focus of interest in the beach as a social and recreational space. Gymnastics, sea-bathing and water-based activities such as water-skiing suddenly became popular. As it happened, Florence Gould was at the forefront of promoting this latter activity, and was herself an ardent and capable participant. Also a keen tennis player, she even arranged for the French Ladies Champion, Suzanne Lenglen, to give her lessons on the courts at Le Provençal.

In a recent exhibition, entitled *'Art Deco Budapest: Posters, Lifestyle and the City'* (2022) the social changes described above were summarized as follows:

'In the aftermath of the First World War, it became more common for women, even those from middle classes, to take on paid employment, and this led to a fundamental change in gender roles. The new ideal for women in the 1920s was no longer the figure hidden in the cage of matrimony and the home, but the woman who moved casually in the public sphere, making a show of her modernity: the young, slim woman with boyishly short hair, the garçonne or flapper.

The more active lifestyle also changed women's fashion, with modern garments giving women more freedom of movement; the corset, for instance, disappeared, and skirts became shorter. Due to the new fashion, much more of the female body was revealed, no longer confined by a corset, so modern women struggled to stay slim through diet and exercise. The beach and bathing culture became part of the health cult and legitimised the display of the almost naked body, even on posters.

The female face also appeared in a new light; make up had previously been associated with immorality and women of ill repute, but between the wars it gained a place in the lives of the respectable, middle-class, modern woman'.

Furthermore, these trends:

'... provided more and more opportunities for entertainment, and with the growing popularity of restaurants, theatres, nightclubs, and concerts, elegant attire became more and more visible than ever before.

The new dances, too, shaped the ball gowns; as the fast movements made the glittering, hanging ornaments even more prominent, the barely knee-length dresses used for the Charleston and other dances in the mid-1920s were often decorated with heavy embroidery and fringes of beads and sequins.'

In the face of these radical changes in life-styles, Gould quickly turned his attention to marketing Juan as *the* place to be, and to be seen. In this, he, and others, were more than successful. A once meagre settlement was not only at the forefront in terms

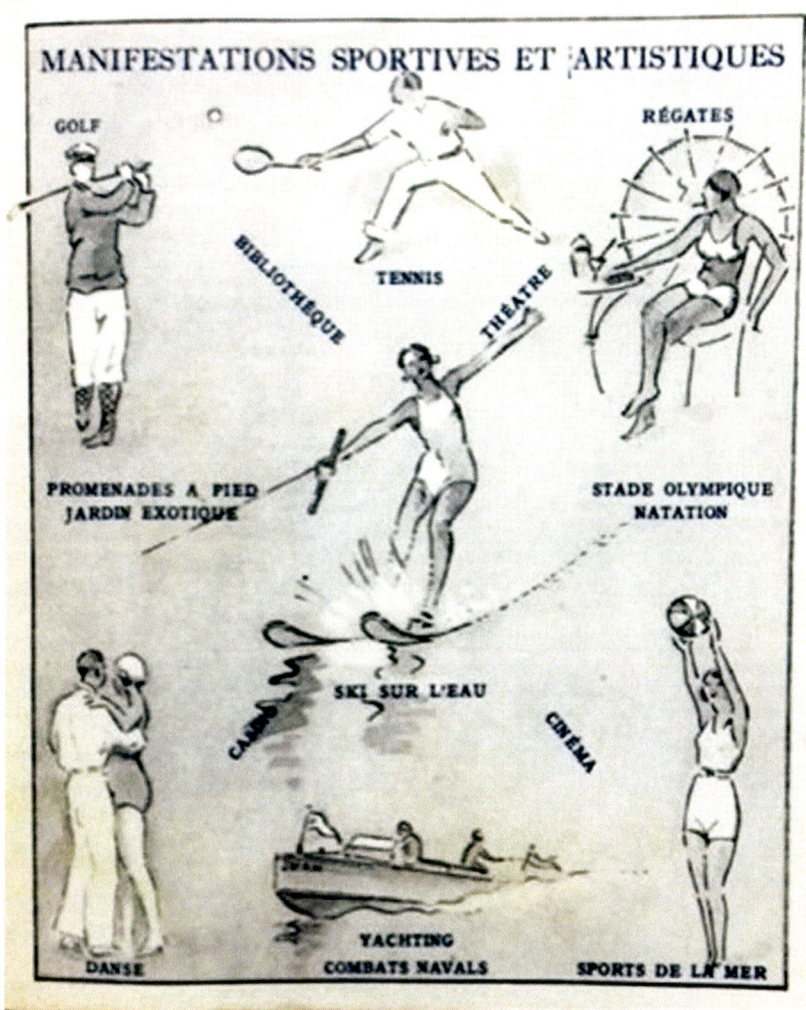

Publicity Brochure

promoting the summer season on the Riviera. It would soon become known internationally as somewhere where freedom of expression was most clearly on display. Inevitably, it was not long before celebrities from the world of stage and screen would find time to pay a visit. Hollywood stars, in particular, would take up residence in Le Provençal, where Florence would often be holding forth with her usual élan. Others, perhaps a little more abstemious in behaviour would choose to rest up in the nearby Grand Hôtel du Cap. If they assumed that in so doing they could escape the madding crowd they were to be quickly disabused. Even there, high jinks were becoming more and more par for the course; sometimes embarrassingly so. Needless to say, not everyone was happy with the new order. Likewise, Anne de Courcy in a biography entitled *'Chanel's Riviera'*, expressed the view that:

> *'There was no doubt, however, that the epicentre of the mélange of high life and low morals that characterised so many of the summer crowd was Antibes'.*

In so saying, she was presumably referring to Juan-les-Pins rather than specifically to the town of Antibes itself.

The growing number of visitors to Juan-les-Pins may have pleased the Goulds, but it inevitably put pressure on Cap d'Antibes. In particular, it brought the locality into wider prominence and boosted interest in residential development. It also meant that more and more people would be exploring its interior and gathering on its coves and small and more intimate beaches. The rapidly changing social scene was certainly not to the liking of the Murphys as they relaxed in Villa America. In a letter to Zelda Fitzgerald, who had returned to America for a short stay, Sara wrote: *'People have now started to crowd onto our beach (La Garoupe)'*; adding, dismissively, that those now descending on the area tended to be *'nouveaux riches'* rather than creative artists. The *'old intimacy'*, as she was to put it, *'had ebbed'*. Despite this, the Murphys stayed on and continued to invite friends and to entertain as impeccably as ever. But it was not to last. The stock market crash in 1929 and the Great Depression that came in its slipstream soon impacted on their assets, as it did on so many others. With family concerns also causing problems, the Murphys were obliged to rethink their situation. In the end the decision was taken to sell Villa America and to sever close ties with the Côte d'Azur once and for all. A short-lived, but immensely colourful and creative episode in the social history of the whole locality had come to an end.

Cap d'Antibes in particular was visibly no longer what it once was. More and more villas set in substantial grounds were under construction, encroaching relentlessly on plots once cultivated, and on areas under natural vegetation. According to one source, in 1895 there were estimated to be 45 large villas on the cape; by the early 1930s the number was thought to be over 200. But not everyone who figured in the heady days of the 1920s decided to move on. The Goulds were among them. Despite their expanding business interests in Nice and elsewhere, the couple remained committed to Juan. It was there in 1956 that Frank Gould died, aged 78. As one obituary observed *'he turned the quiet backwater of Juan-les-Pins into a famed international spa'*. Florence was to live on until 1983. She was 88 when she passed away, spending her final years in Cannes at her new villa – El Patio. As the New York Times was to report, for 25 years she sumptuously entertained, *'surrounded by her Impressionist paintings, 18th-century French clocks and furniture, English silver, Gothic and Renaissance objects and artist-illustrated books'*.[17] However, in certain quarters her social standing was to be tarnished by her dubious connections with the German hierarchy during the Second World War. In the minds of some, there was more than a whiff of collusion. Whatever the truth of this particular matter there is no doubt that, in her later years, she supported numerous charitable organizations. Of the many larger-than-life personalities who had made their presence felt in Juan and indeed in the wider locality, few could be said to have matched the Goulds. But there were many others who also left indelible imprints. *'Les Années Folles'* had come to an end. But it was fun while it lasted.

2
Villa Eilenroc: Family Sagas

Introduction

There was a slight edge to the offshore wind as the French writer and sailing enthusiast, Guy de Maupassant, made his way down to the harbour at Antibes on an early April morning in the mid 1880s. In his quasi-diary, which was later to be published under the title *'Sur l'eau'*, he recalls that within the bounding walls of the old garrison town all was quiet, except, that is, for the sound of a few dogs rummaging around in the narrow streets and dark alleyways. There were some early risers about, mainly on their way to work, but they were few in number. The sun was rising, the darkness was lifting, but everything still seemed somnolent *'under the gold-spangled firmament'*.[1] Maupassant was light-hearted and looking forward to what lay ahead; for he was about to board his small, beloved yacht, the *Bel Ami* by name, for a languid week-long excursion along the coast. He would be in convivial company, for joining him on board was his ever-watchful skipper, Bernard, together with a swarthy crewmate – Raymond. The weather appeared to be set fair, and Maupassant was soon in a reflective and somewhat discursive frame of mind.

Having negotiated their way through the medley of bobbing craft within the port, the sailing party headed out into the open sea. Here, the breeze steadily freshened and the small craft quickly gathered pace, *'skimming over the quivering violet-tinted waters'*. *Bel Ami*

Guy de Maupassant

soon rounded the headland of Cap d'Antibes and entered *La Baie de Golfe Juan*. From there, Maupassant looked out on a coastal scene in which villas, largely owned by people from foreign parts, had by now become a prominent feature both on the shoreline and on the hillsides behind.

'And everywhere, all along the endless coast, the towns by the seashore, the villages perched up on high on the mountain side, the innumerable villas dotted about in the greenery, all look like white eggs laid on the sand, laid on the rocks, laid amongst the pine forests by gigantic birds that have come in the night from the snowfields far above'.

Before sailing on towards Cannes and the offshore *Iles de Lérins*, Maupassant gazed back wistfully at the headland they had just skirted. He knew Cap d'Antibes well. Over the years he had often explored its rural interior and rocky coastal fringes. It was clearly dear to his heart, for he considered the whole cape to be *'a wonderful garden thrown out between the seas, blooming with the most beautiful flowers of Europe'*. Also catching his eye, at the tip of the cape, there stood an imposing villa, which he called Ellen-Roc (sic), and which he considered to be *'a charming and whimsical residence*'; one that was attracting admiring visitors, especially excursionists from the neighbouring and burgeoning resorts of Cannes and Nice.

Coincidentally, at around the very time that Maupassant was based in Antibes, so too was Stéphen Liégeard. He was busy collecting information for his soon to be published tome. In it, he would have no hesitation in lauding Ellen-Roc as a veritable gem, a pearl no less – *'la perle du Golfe'*. In his view it was also a singularly welcoming place, where the visitor was permitted to wander at will, and where, he claimed, perhaps a little too fulsomely, nightingales nested in clumps of aromatic chamomile (*Anthemis*) and geraniums. The villa itself, with its marmoreal façade, reminded him of ancient Greece. And this, despite the fact that the marble used was, as he typically phrased it, from Carrara in Tuscany rather than the island of Paros in the Cyclades! From its balustraded terrace, those arriving could look out over the secluded *Baie des Milliardaires* and the wider *Anse de l'Argent Faux*. All in all, it was a truly enchanting scene. In his text, Liégeard also draws his readers' attention to the stone steps (apparently 67 in all) that led precipitously down into a cove that opened up a whole new world, far removed from the tended gardens some 30 metres above. Here, the crystal-clear sea, in its more tempestuous moments, had deeply pitted and gouged the red rock formations, and carved out grottoes, platforms and small embayments. In a myriad of nooks and crannies, agaves, myrtle and cistus were able to sustain themselves, and render a wild tropical feel to the sun-drenched enclave. Viewed as an ensemble, Liégeard was moved to propose that along the coast there was no other place to match that of Ellen-Roc (henceforth Eilenroc); not even the *'Trianon'* within the grounds of the Palace of Versailles.[2] Thereafter, many other commentators would think likewise. Praise indeed, for there were many other elegant villas and associated *'domaines'* (estates) along the littoral of the Riviera that could make claim to be serious contenders.

Whilst Maupassant makes no mention of the owner, Liégeard does briefly refer to a certain Mr. Wyllie, who (as is commonly the case among French writers at this time, and indeed thereafter) he erroneously states was an Englishman. He was in fact Scottish. James Wyllie (see below) was indubitably the key early figure in the shaping of Eilenroc, but he was not the first to identify the uniqueness and potential of the site.

Up until the middle part of the 19th century Cap d'Antibes was very much a world unto itself. Guarded by the garrison town of Antibes, with its walls, bastions and ramparts, the cape was a patchily cultivated realm, with only limited and scattered habitation. Here and there, smallholdings devoted to the tending of cereals, vines, olives and fig trees were intermixed with intensive market gardening that yielded salad crops and much more for neighbouring settlements. Floriculture was a particularly prominent feature, with the production of carnations (*oeillets*) coming increasingly to the fore. Habitation, such as it then was, was dominantly of a basic rustic order – vernacular farmhouses, cottages and rudimentary cabins dotted the landscape. Beyond the areas under cultivation were tracts of rough Mediterranean vegetation (*garrigues*). Along the wind-swept coastal fringes twisted Aleppo pines and maritime flora added variety to the scene. In parts, especially across the southern extremity of the cape, thick clusters of Parasol (stone) pines – *Pinus pinea* – gave shade and warm redolence. Movement within the cape itself was dependent upon a network of rough tracks, footpaths (*sentiers*) and bridleways. They served not only those living and working in the immediate area (*Antibois*). Increasingly, they were taken full advantage of by visitors from neighbouring parts, and particularly so at weekends for leisurely outings *'en famille'*. An especially popular vantage point was the 75 metres high summit of the limestone plateau (*Plâteau de la Garoupe*), clothed in *chênes verts* (evergreen oaks), on which the lighthouse and the *Église Notre Dame de la Garoupe* stood. For those who had ventured to clamber their breathless way up the steep rocky path – '*Le Chemin du Calvaire*', the panoramic views were reward enough.

At around the time that Maupassant and Liégeard were wandering there, the wider commune of Antibes mustered approximately 7,000 souls. But few were permanent residents of the cape *per se*, and even these were scattered in distribution. In this demographic sense alone, it was truly a realm unto itself.

The Founding Years

A quiet backwater of local interest it may have long been, but by the middle part of the 19th century Cap d'Antibes suddenly caught the attention of those seeking out locations for upmarket residential development. In this regard, the Côte d'Azur was becoming increasingly popular as a place of winter resort, with representatives of the European Gotha in particular gracing the locality with their esteemed and moneyed presence. They were looking for places of standing – hotels and villas – where they could rest up for a while. Many of them would be suffering from sundry ailments (most notably pulmonary tuberculosis), which they hoped would be eased by the warm and soothing Mediterranean clime. On hand were doctors from all over Europe. They were only too ready to cater for their sundry medical needs. For them, it was a lucrative clientele. But over time ever increasing numbers would arrive seeking to indulge themselves in more worldly pleasures. Interestingly, the property developers who first sought to satisfy the emerging residential demand were not local, nor, by and large, French. The majority arrived from far-flung parts of northern Europe. Elsewhere along the coast, most notably in Cannes and Nice, British speculators and private investors had held early sway. But, as far as Cap d'Antibes was concerned, almost from the outset it was two interlinked Russian families, the Fersens and Plestcheyeffs, who were particularly significant players (see 3). However, many of their early forays into the market failed to materialize, at least to the extent that they had first envisaged.

James Close

During the 1860s a notable first-time visitor to the area, James Close, had similar ideas concerning the promotion and development of the cape as a place worthy of settlement. English, he had spent a formative part of his career in Italy, first in Sicily and then in Naples where he quickly established a reputation for himself as a 'merchant' in the field of banking and investment. Such was the high esteem in which he was held, that he became a financial advisor to King Ferdinand II. In 1859, on the death of the King, Close elected to retire and to move with his large family (six sons and three daughters), together with his yacht *Sibella*, to the South of France. He settled for Antibes, with its sheltered harbour proving to be an added attraction. Having failed, like Lord Brougham (the earlier developer of Cannes), in his endeavour to purchase the nearby residence that had at one time been home to the Bonaparte family – *Château Salé*, he chose to buy 17 hectares of land on the Cap, and spent a small fortune on the construction of a commodious villa. At the same time he drew up plans for the development of a cluster of similarly luxurious residences in the immediate locality. Unfortunately, his sudden death, following a heart attack in 1865, meant that his vision for the area – as a select and exclusive domain – was not to be realised.

As it happened, that very same year, work was started on the construction of the villa to be named Eilenroc, which some twenty years later would so impress Maupassant and Liégeard. In recounting the history of that particular residence, reference needs to be made to four very different families who were to contribute to its development and fame. Collectively, the lives of those concerned could hardly be described as staid or uneventful – far from it. They were convoluted in the extreme, and most certainly characterful. In their very different ways, and over varying periods of time, they would all leave their particular footprints.

The ill-fated Loudon family

Eilenroc was one of a suite of significant residences to be established on the wooded southern fringe of Cap d'Antibes. It was Hugh Hope Loudon who first purchased the prime coastal site on which the villa was to be constructed. Although he was born in the coastal settlement of Semarang in Central Java (Dutch East Indies at that time, now officially the Republic of Indonesia) in 1818 and was, therefore, Dutch, his father – Alexander – actually hailed from the small settlement of Tannadice in Scotland. He had joined the British Navy in 1811 and was at one point based on the island of Java. Whether or not it was there or back in Holland that he first met her is not certain, but it is known that in 1818 he married Suzanna Gaspardine Valk. She came from the town of Kampen, some 90 kilometres from Amsterdam, and at the time was just 17 years old.

Over the years to come, Alexander built up commercial interests in the Dutch East Indies, and quickly amassed a fortune for himself as a refiner of sugar and manufacturer of indigo. In the meantime, Suzanna was equally busy producing offspring – seven in all. Although Hugh Hope, their first child, was born while the couple were living in Java, his brothers (there were no sisters) were all born back in Holland. In 1824, with his business interests becoming even more deeply rooted in the Dutch East Indies, Alexander decided to adopt Dutch nationality. Their children were often placed in the care of Suzanna's grandmother, whilst the couple would make return visits to Java, overseeing their various business interests.

Tragically, it was during one such trip in 1828 that Suzanna died, aged 27. At the time they were resident at the coastal settlement of Rembang. Despondent, her husband returned home, but only survived her by a further two years. He died in Rotterdam in 1830, aged 41, leaving a substantial legacy.

Hugh Hope Loudon was just 12 years old when his father passed away. Details as to his education and career are limited. He clearly spent time in Java, his place of birth, but as to how long he was there and what he did in terms of employment is not known. It is commonly suggested that he worked in the colonial service, possibly even rising to the rank of governor. What *is* certain, however, is that while there he met Paulina Ignatia de Kock van Leeuwen. Also of Dutch stock, she was born on the island in 1826. The couple married in the early 1840s, and in 1844 they had their first and only child – John Francis Loudon. Just two years later, however, aged 20, Paulina also died. Colonial living in tropical parts had a lot to answer for.

It would be many more years before Hugh would remarry. This he did in the late 1850s. His new wife was a baroness from the Friesland district in the Netherlands – Wilhelmina Cornelia van Pallandt. Their first two children were girls – Constantia Alexine in 1859 and Suzanna Helena in 1861. Some four years later, while looking for a second home to be used as a winter retreat, the couple came across the singular site on which they would soon set about building the villa that would be called Eilenroc for ever more. It is commonly recounted in the literature that the name given to the property was Hugh's wife's Christian name in reverse form – an anagram, as some would have it. In fact, as cited, her first name was Wilhelmina. Furthermore, to her family she was known as 'Jacoba'. Admittedly, her second name comes close, but as stated it was Cornelia not Cornélie. Such matters are of little consequence, apart from anecdotally, and possibly her husband did indeed call her such. Perhaps being in France simply made it a more appropriate appellation. Be all this as it may, the couple embarked on the preparatory task of having the land cleared and leveled. The next stage involved the construction of the residence itself. Although a few have queried the fact, seemingly for want of definitive documentary evidence, it is often claimed that the celebrated architect Charles Garnier drew up the plans for the Loudon's neo-classical residence.[3]

If so, then Loudon was fortunate indeed to gain his services, for Garnier was exceedingly busy and pre-occupied at that time. Indeed, between 1861 and 1875, he was immersed in the design and construction of the famed Paris Opéra (later commonly referred to as the *Palais Garnier*). Whatever the truth of the matter, with building works continuing apace, the villa itself was completed in 1867. A year on, the Loudons extended their family with the birth in 1868 of James Hope. Their last child – Willem Constantijn – arrived five years later. On the family front, all may have looked well, but behind the scenes the marriage was clearly failing, for the couple were to part, no doubt acrimoniously. For all concerned, no longer did Eilenroc have the familial appeal that it once had.

Despite all the effort and resources that had been invested, the decision was taken to sell the *'domaine'*. If he did so with a heavy heart, then Hugh must have gained some comfort from the fact that the next owner of his exquisite but unfinished villa would come from the very same part of Scotland as his father, Alexander.

Charles Garnier

Eilenroc – Early Stages of Development

Years of Consolidation: James and Helen Wyllie

James Wyllie took ownership of Villa Eilenroc in 1873. He was born in 1819 in Montrose, a vibrant port town on the east coast of Scotland.[4] At the time it had a population of some 10,000 and was a significant sea trading centre, dealing in goods from all parts of the world. The wealth generated was manifest in the impressive solidity of its merchants' houses, while the town's global commercial links were formally recognized in street names, many of which are extant. Of the latter, 'India Street' would resonate with Wyllie's future commercial and trading interests, although they would in due course be directed not from Montrose but from Liverpool – then a major centre of mercantile activity that was rivalled only by London, and to which the Wyllies moved to widen opportunities.

In the meantime, it was in Montrose that James would court

and then marry Helen Keith. She lived in the nearby coastal village of St Cyrus. There, in 1848, the couple exchanged vows. James was 29, while Helen's age goes unrecorded. Whether or not they were then based in Liverpool is unclear, but soon after their marriage they are known to have moved to Calcutta (now Kolkata) where James pursued commercial opportunities in the textile trade. There, the couple set up home in the select part of the Chowringhee district known as White town. It was also at around this time that James succeeded in sealing a business deal that would see his own merchant company becoming a division of a much bigger enterprise, based in Liverpool and belonging to the go-getting John Gladstone.[5]

In Calcutta, the Wyllies prospered and entered fully into the vibrant cultural life of the town, becoming active members of the expatriate community. As devout Christians they attended services in the recently built St Paul's Cathedral. Opened in 1847, the driving force behind its construction was the then presiding bishop, Daniel Wilson. Wyllie clearly impressed the bishop, for an entry in Wilson's journal makes glowing reference to his new congregant. In it, he says of Wyllie that he is *'one of those noble, kind-hearted, thoroughly good men, of whom there are so few in the world'*. Sadly, such magnanimity went unrewarded on a personal front, for while residing in Calcutta, the couple were to suffer the loss at birth of two sons – James in 1849 and David two years later. Perhaps it was this that caused them to return home. But if, in so doing, they were hoping for a change in the fortunes of the family, they were to be sorely disappointed, for in 1853, when they were living in West Derby, a then affluent part of suburban Liverpool, yet another son was to die at birth – Alexander.

Little is known of the Wyllies in the years that followed, but they were clearly on their travels again, for in February 1856 it was recorded that they had stopped over in Malta, and that in Sliema, a district adjoining the capital Valetta, Helen gave birth to a girl. After having already lost three sons, the couple must have been overjoyed. Taking her mother's first name, Helen was destined to lead a highly charged life, much of which would be acted out on Cap d'Antibes. For it was there in 1873 that they purchased Eilenroc. The villa would become a second home for the much-travelled family: a place to which they could retreat and graciously entertain honoured guests, particularly during clement winter months. Their residency in Eilenroc would last for many years. Apparently, no thought was given to changing the name of the villa.

Whilst they could move into their new home forthwith, having agreed to buy the furnishings from Hugh Loudon, there was clearly much to be done, not least as far as the grounds were concerned. For one reason or another, Loudon would appear not to have invested much effort in the landscaping of the site – no doubt, towards the end of his time there, he had other more pressing personal matters with which to contend. By and large, the terrain remained in its raw semi-natural state, and was not an appropriate setting for a villa of such reputed architectural pedigree. To do justice to the place, Wyllie called in a highly respected garden designer based locally, with Albert Ringuisan often being cited. Under his supervision, the scrub was cleared, topsoil brought in, pathways laid out, and plantings configured. Within no time at all, Eilenroc was gaining a commendable reputation for itself. And all the more so when Wyllie proposed that, on payment of a modest consideration, the grounds, now covering some 11 hectares, would be open to visitors twice a week. Ever the philanthropist, Wyllie directed the sums thus garnered to the municipality of Antibes, specifically in munificent support of local social causes.[6] Liégeard, in his tome, pointedly noted that other *'domaines'* on the cape did not follow suit. Interestingly, he makes no mention of a token charitable payment; indicating that all that was necessary for entry was for the would-be visitor to sign a register.[7] In his text Liégeard also refers to the two hedges that line the main pathway to the villa as *'deux haies de bengales'* (two Bengal hedges). He was clearly aware of the proprietor's Indian credentials!

Eilenroc – A Walkway

Walkway and Balustrade

Such was the high esteem in which the Wyllies were held, that over the years they welcomed an array of prominent visitors to their estate. Included among them was the Conservative statesman Lord Salisbury – three times British Prime Minister and four times Foreign Secretary. In so doing Salisbury did not have to travel far, since he had his own winter retreat further along the coast at Beaulieu-sur-Mer. Called *'La Bastide'*, he had acquired the villa in 1892. It was while sojourning there that he welcomed Queen Victoria to his winter retreat. Another political figure of particular eminence paying a visit was Lord Gladstone. Needless to say, given Wyllie's business links with Gladstone's father back in Liverpool, he would most certainly have been an especially honoured guest.

Entrance to Eilenroc

Eilenroc: Grottoes and Coastal Promenade

But it was not just those formally invited to the villa that attested to the high regard in which Eilenroc was increasingly held. Reference to one of the visitors' books reveals an astonishing array of notable day visitors who made their way to Cap d'Antibes from elsewhere along the coast. They walked the grounds of the villa, and presumably looked out admiringly from its terrace at the wide expanse of azure sea before them, with the purple-red igneous rocks (porphyry) of the Esterel Massif in the far distance. Some may even have ventured down the precipitous flight of steps to the coves and grottoes below.

Interestingly, in 2015 the auction house Vitber Art & Antiques advertised the sale of a guestbook from Eilenroc.[8] As part of the supporting promotional literature, a list was provided of some of the more prominent autographs to be found within. Admittedly, the auction house concerned is based in Riga, the capital city of Latvia, which presumably biased the selection of names from the list of many, but the number of titled Russians who found time to visit Eilenroc, whilst over-wintering on the Riviera, is impressive. Those cited included: Empress Maria Feodorovna, wife of Tsar Alexander III; Grand Duke Konstantin Nikolaevich, together with his wife, Grand Duchess Alexandra Josephovna (*sic*); Grand Duke Nicholas Nikolaevich the Elder; the daughter of Nicholas I and sister of Emperor Alexander II, Olga Nikolaevna. Also registered are numerous Russian princes, princesses, counts and countesses, barons and baronesses, not to mention sundry maids of honour. The Russians apart, other guest books also contained signatures and laudatory comments from a vast array of eminences, including members of the wider European Gotha, political figures, as well as many from the world of fashion, literature, dance and art. For someone who started out life in a small Scottish town, and who had worked so hard to build a successful trading business in India, to have so many personages of such standing finding the time to visit his house and gardens must have been flattering in the extreme. But James Wyllie was not a self-focused or self-aggrandizing individual, and was able to put such vainglorious matters into a wider Christian perspective. His generosity in regard to the needy of the locality bore ample testimony to that.

Eilenroc Guestbook

A Period of Chaos and Confusion

At the time, an issue of particular concern to James Wyllie and his wife, was the future of their one and only daughter. When the Wyllies first took possession of Eilenroc, Helen was 17 years of age. She was in her mid-twenties when, presumably back in London, she met and fell for Hugh Coleridge Downing Kennard, the son of Coleridge Kennard, Member of Parliament for Salisbury and co-founder of the Evening News newspaper. Hughie, as she lovingly addressed him, was in the military and had attained the rank of lieutenant in the Grenadier Guards. After the customary formal agreements had been reached, attention now turned to financial matters. They reputedly included a gift of £50,000 plus securities to Helen from her father, together with an annual allowance of £3,000. Coleridge John Kennard confirmed a reciprocal financial package for his son. James Wyllie duly gave his approval to the marriage. Delighted and excited, Helen wrote, somewhat deferentially, to her prospective father-in-law that:

> 'The future seems too bright, almost too good to be true! For I love Hughie with all my heart and long for the time when I can devote my life to make his a happy one and pray and trust that I may succeed.'

The couple married in 1883, and set up home in London. Their substantial residence was located in Hans Place – the much sought-after 18th century garden square, located close to Hyde Park. Money was clearly of little concern, and all seemed to be going well on the conjugal front; particularly so when, two years later, in April 1885, Helen gave birth to a son – the grandly named Coleridge Arthur Fitzroy Kennard. Later, friends would simply refer to him familiarly as 'Roy'. If there was delight in the household, and in the family at large, then it was to be short-lived, for relations between the couple rapidly soured, and to a point where they were leading increasingly separate lives. Wishing to explore avenues new, Hugh would frequently take time out in order to 'do his own thing'. It was on just such an occasion that tragedy struck. On a lone trip abroad, he seemingly got into difficulties while swimming and drowned. As to precisely where and how the accident happened is not clear. Equally unclear is Helen's reaction. Undoubtedly there would have been considerable shock expressed, but perhaps this was tempered by awareness that the future of their relationship looked bleak anyway.

Hugh Kennard died on 9th April 1886, and was just 26 years of age. Hugh's mother (Ellen Georgiana) took his death particularly badly and over the coming years insisted on wearing black. Her class-conscious spirits were to be raised, however, following the award of a baronetcy to her husband in 1890. The mourning dress was duly shed. But not for long; for within that year her husband had also died – on Christmas Day no less. He was 62 years old. Although the award of a baronetcy to her husband had not been formally gazetted, after much lobbying and by royal warrant, Georgiana (as she was normally called) was herself later granted *'the ranking, style and precedence'* of the wife of a baronet – a title that she had so long cherished. But it was to be her only grandson who would be accorded the patent of 1st Baronet. This was in February 1901. Roy was then just five years of age.

Seeking to come to terms with it all, Helen sought a degree of solace in Eilenroc, with her parents presumably on hand to help out, as she embarked upon the task of watching over the development of her infant, and now fatherless, son. But she would not have to do so for long, since Roy would soon be enrolled as a boarder in Eton College. In the meantime Helen had met James Carew, a Member of Parliament and committed Irish nationalist. Both in their early 40s, they married in 1896. If she thought that her life was now finally gaining a degree of stability, and respectability, then once again she would be disabused. The year 1903 could not have been worse, for in August her beloved father, James – the assured and benevolent patriarch of the family, and the one who had laid the foundations for its material well-being, suddenly died. At the time he had been living in quiet retirement on the south coast of England in Brighton (Hove). He was aged 84. As if that were not enough for Helen to cope with, in October of the same year, when they were holidaying in St Moritz, Switzerland, and with Roy in tow, her new husband also passed away. They had been wed for just seven years. To Helen the future must have looked desolate indeed. All that she now had to look forward to on the family front rested with her son. At 18 Roy was the future legatee of his grandfather's estate, a prized component of which was Eilenroc.

Wildean Associations

As far as the family's longer-term hold on Eilenroc was concerned, much depended upon whether or not Roy would continue to show sufficient interest in the property, and the degree to which he would consider it to be a key part of his substantial portfolio of assets. That he held fond memories of his childhood years there is certain, for he would state as much in one of his later writings (see below). At first, all seemed hopeful. With Helen around to advise him, and not short of liquidity, there was little to suggest that he might wish to sell the place. After Eton, his mind was focused on settling into a career. This he duly did, following in his father's footsteps by joining the Grenadier Guards. However, with life in the military proving not to be to his liking, in 1909 he abruptly switched, and secured a position in the Diplomatic Service. A high-flying progression within the Foreign Office now seemed assured. But then, a number of controversial and well-publicised incidents occurred, which raised questions as to Roy's lifestyle and personal probity. They also drew his mother into the imbroglio. It all happened so very quickly.

Contentious issues first arose within a year of Roy having taken up his position as an aspiring diplomat, but had started innocently enough a few years earlier in 1904, and seemingly as a result of a portrait by the French painter – Jacques-Émile Blanche (1861-1942). Highly regarded in Parisian circles, Blanche had been awarded the commission by Helen, with a view to capturing her son's essence. As it turned out, the resulting portrait was most certainly not to her liking. What upset Roy's mother so much was that, in her view, the artist had depicted her adored son as being somewhat effete and foppish. In particular, it was the long, slender hands of the sitter, and the all-too languid pose, that aroused her motherly ire. Such was Helen's indignation that she insisted that the painting should never be placed on public display. It was not until many years later, in 1924, that she finally relented, but only on condition that her son's name should in no way be attached to the work of art. According to one source, Roy himself later explained to Blanche, no doubt somewhat apologetically, that his mother did not appreciate the portrait because, in her view, it was far too tendentious as to her son's *'mode de vie'*.[9]

The painting, which is now in a private collection, had originally been baldly titled: *'Sir Coleridge Kennard sitting on a sofa'*. Given the sensitive background to the dispute, a renaming was deemed desirable. Henceforth, it was to be referred to as *'Le Portrait de*

Coleridge Kennard by J-E Blanche

Coleridge Kennard in 1924

Dorian Grey'. Needless to say, the implied association (accidental or otherwise) between her son and the sensualist character in Oscar Wilde's novel '*Dorian Grey*' was doubly ironic, for Helen had long been a close friend and admirer of the author. And this despite the fact that in 1895, and for a two-year period, Wilde had been imprisoned for having committed acts of gross indecency. So why, it may well be asked, the dissatisfaction with the portrait of her son in the first place? More than that, she had also taken a keen interest in the development of Wilde's two sons – Vyvyan and Cyril, following the death of their mother, Constance in 1898. In the face of indignant public disapproval, Constance had felt that a change of family name was more than desirable. Henceforth, it would be Holland.

Although controversial, Helen ensured that Wilde's two boys would come to know and appreciate their father's literary works. Inevitably, her own son, Roy, who was the same age as Cyril, became a close friend of the brothers. On his release from prison, Oscar Wilde moved to France, and would apparently never see his children again. On a number of occasions he would visit the Côte d'Azur, especially Cannes, where he would meet up with his friend and supporter, the infamous Frank Harris, who owned a property nearby. Interestingly, in terms of coincidental linkages, Harris had at one time served as an editor of the Evening News – the paper once owned by Helen's former father-in-law – George Kennard.

Such was Helen's belief in Wilde's genius that she later contributed significantly to the fund set up by his friend Robert Rosse, specifically to commission a suitably dramatic headstone for his grave in the *Cimetière de Père Lachaise* in Paris. It was to there in 1909 that his remains were to be transferred from their original place of burial in Bagneux, a district located to the south of the city. The headstone was designed by Sir Jacob Epstein and, perhaps not unexpectedly, would prove to be somewhat controversial; largely because of its priapic physicality.

It would be interesting to know if any members of the Wilde

(Holland) family or associated friends ever visited Eilenroc. If they did so, one can only imagine what the church-going James Wyllie would have thought of it all. No doubt he would have been turning, politely but somewhat disconcertedly, in his grave back on the south coast of England. Little detail seems to be available concerning the comings and goings at Eilenroc during this time.

'Roy' Kennard – Chaotic Relationships

The indelicate issue of the 'Dorian Grey' painting, his mother's longstanding concern for the well-being of Oscar Wilde's children, together with the efforts she made to ensure that his contributions to literature were more widely recognized, did not appear to have a direct impact upon Roy Kennard's standing in society. Much more damaging was his increasingly wayward behaviour. Problems on this front were first manifest soon after he embarked on his career as an attaché in the Foreign Office. A cause for particular comment early on was his openly espoused infatuation with a married woman. Not only that, she also happened to be a mother of two. It was far from being *'comme il faut'*. To make matters worse, Roy was apparently insisting that the lady concerned should leave her family forthwith; otherwise, he informed her in writing, he would not hesitate to commit suicide. It was all too much – wholly beyond the social pale.

The lady in question was bright, attractive and adventurous, but seen by some – fallaciously so – as a mere fortune hunter. That said, she would most certainly have loved Eilenroc. From lowly stock, she was born in Hungary to a British father and Polish mother. They were seemingly of very limited means. Somehow or other, in 1877, at the age of 12, she had been sent to England to further her education. Later, as a young adult, she spent time socializing on the fringes of high society in London. It was there in 1896, that Yoï, as she was known to friends, met and subsequently married, a certain Captain James Buckley.[10] She was then aged 19. On her marriage certificate her full name was recorded as Cornelia Edith Yoï Crosse – yet another Cornelia enters the frame! As for James Buckley, he was the owner of a landed estate in Carmarthenshire (Wales), and of a successful brewery business. Furthermore, in the locality at least, he was a man of considerable standing. Having been brought up in a remote part of Hungary where her family had struggled to make even a meagre living from the tending of vines, Yoï seemingly had little difficulty settling down in West Wales, in what was a wet, relatively remote, and socially constrained, chapel-going part of the world. What she thought of the widespread use of the Welsh language is not known. But it was there that the couple set about happily building a family and managing their estate. Two sons were duly born – Wilma and Gabriel. But then came her unpardonable liaison with Roy. How it came about is not clear, but it may have been as a consequence of Yoï's acquaintance with Oscar Wilde's close friend, Robert Rosse, that, back in London's *'beau monde'*, the pair came to know each other. When the relationship first began, Yoï was by then in her early thirties, while Roy was just 24. It was an intense and urgent affair; for Yoï in particular, divorce was a *sine qua non*.

Mrs Cornelia Buckley

Far from enamoured of the emerging drama, Roy's mother, Helen, quickly sought to nip the unconscionable relationship firmly in the bud. Attracting increasingly vehement comment, it was becoming too much of a social embarrassment. Far better if her son were out of the country – out of sight, and perhaps out of mind. A Foreign Office posting as far away as possible could surely be arranged. She had friends in high places. Such were her connections that Roy was soon on his way to Rome. Fine as a first step, but it did not deter the strong-willed and resourceful Yoï.

Reliant on funds from Roy, and the encouragement of a continual flow of amorous letters from him, Yoï headed off on what would turn out to be a daunting and ultimately fruitless journey, at least as far as her relationship with Roy was concerned. Such was the pressure that was being put on him, and seemingly with doubts creeping into his own mind anyway, Roy was only too pleased to accept yet another 'face-saving' posting, this time to Tehran. Those behind the move may have thought that Yoï would finally see the light and call an end to her increasingly ignoble pursuit. If so, then they were to be disappointed. Having arrived in Rome too late to meet up with Roy, and suffering a serious shortage of funds, she remained resourceful and optimistic. Tehran was now her next target. She was certainly not about to give up and go home.

In Tehran, Roy was already settling into his new position as third secretary to Sir George Head Barclay, who was Envoy Extraordinary and Minister Plenipotentiary to the Shah of Persia. More than that, he was now turning his amorous attention to Sir George's daughter Dorothy. By the time Yoï arrived, weary after an onerous but highly eventful trek, the situation was irretrievable. Persuaded by those around him that his paramour was indeed self-seeking, and no doubt with his ardour cooling anyway, Roy initially refused to see the one who had given up so much for him. Despite a valiant effort on her part, Yoï reluctantly had to accept that she was now pursuing a lost cause. Nonplussed but determined to battle on, she made her way back to Rome. There, resilient as ever, she succeeded in carving out a new and highly successful life for herself.[11]

With Roy now away in Persia, it was presumably up to his mother to oversee the management of the Eilenroc estate. Of this time in its history little would appear to have been written, but it can be assumed that during the first decade of the new century, and following the death of her husband, Helen would have continued to use it as a base for winter stays on the Côte d'Azur. Possibly Roy also found the time to pay occasional visits. The tradition of opening up the gardens to the general public, one must suppose, was also maintained. Helen's father would certainly have wished her to do so. For her, such sojourns on Cap d'Antibes would surely have offered some respite away from the ongoing saga of her son's shambolic start to adult life. But if she hoped that matters would now settle down, she was once again to be disappointed. With Yoï having been peremptorily given her marching orders, the stage was set for yet another messy state of affairs.

It has been noted that on taking up his new position in Tehran, Roy encountered his boss's daughter, Dorothy. The two were soon courting. Not wishing to linger, in

Yoï in Fancy Dress

April 1911 the couple were married. As to Sir George and his wife's feelings on the rushed relationship accounts seem to differ, with some suggesting that they were less than pleased. That the couple threatened to elope, or indeed did elope, did not help matters. Their marriage was reluctantly accepted. Still, for those immediately concerned, the birth of Laurence, the couple's first child, must have raised hopes that in the end all would go well. But it was not to be. The marriage was soon poised on a knife-edge. A second child, George, arrived just after the outbreak of the Great War, but it did not resolve the situation. Apparently making the situation worse was the lingering displeasure at his actions within the Diplomatic Service in Tehran, and within the expatriate community at large. His treatment of Yoï Buckley was deemed by many to be truly reprehensible. It has even been suggested that this was one reason why Sir George himself was soon moved to the embassy in Bucharest, Romania.

But by this time, his daughter's marriage was well and truly over anyway. In due course Dorothy was granted a divorce, with Roy being cited for *'desertion and statutory misconduct'*. In the midst of this marital mayhem he somehow found the wherewithal to travel around Persia and to further his emerging interest in the literature and history of the Middle East. Following the ineluctable collapse of her marriage, Dorothy's life failed to gather any sort of momentum. Her inability to establish a meaningful relationship with her two children also proved to be particularly demoralizing for all concerned. Matters then reached a tragic nadir, when she was paralysed following a car accident. If all that had gone before was not enough, she was destined to spend her last 15 years in a mental institution. Despite her condition, she was to outlive her former husband. Dorothy died in 1953.

Perhaps not surprisingly, come the end of the war, Roy had had his fill of the Diplomatic Service and devoted himself increasingly to his more artistic and avant-garde pursuits, including the writing of poetry and other musings. It would appear that rather than return home, Roy stayed on in Persia for a while, and furthered his deepening interest in Middle Eastern poetry. It has been suggested that during this time he became heavily addicted to narcotics and gambling, and that the impact on his finances was such that he was obliged to sell Villa Eilenroc. Documentary evidence as to the precise nature of the sale, and the reasons that lay behind it, would again appear to be lacking; but what is certain is that the long-term guardianship of the villa by the Wyllie family had come to an end.

Concerning the background to the transaction some observations are made in a very unusual book, published in 1928 and entitled *'The Coast of Pleasure'*.[12] In terms of its content and style, it can hardly be said to be conservative in nature. The fact that the author, Grant Richards, dedicates his text to his 'playmates' says it all. Roy may even have read it! At one point Richards notes:

> *'As at Juan-les-Pins, the value of land on the Cap has soared recently to undreamt-of heights. Take Eileen-Roc (sic), for instance, the late James Wylie's (sic) beautiful property. Worried by the demands of the French income-tax officials, James Wylie's successor not long ago sold it – for something not much over a million francs. That was since the War, of course. Later its purchasers put it up for auction. It was knocked down for twenty-two and a half million. That James Wylie had an eye for beautiful country. Most of the Cap was his until he sold half of it to Mr. Charles Maclaren, now Lord Aberconway, who built La Garoupe, one of the show places of the whole Riviera'.*

Suggesting that the Wyllies laid claim to half of the Cap is clearly an exaggeration, but the reference to the construction and subsequent development of La Garoupe, as he called it, is discussed later. It too is an out-of-the ordinary tale to tell, with another Wales-based family and a Russian oligarch prominently to the fore (see 5).

The dispensing of their prized asset, and one that had figured so centrally in their lives, must have been a wrench for both Roy and his mother. It held so many memories. The above reference apart, the condition of the domain at the time of the sale would appear not to have attracted much comment. What is known, however, is that in order not to sever ties completely with his former home, Roy secured a small corner of the domain on which he arranged for a much more modest residence to be built. Not only that. His spirits were undoubtedly lifted as a result of a new and promising personal relationship – one that would soon lead to yet another marriage in 1924.

This time, his wife-to-be, Mary Graham Orr-Lewis, was the daughter of the prominent Canadian businessman, Sir Frederick Orr-Lewis. He too had been created a baronet in 1920, an honour that was awarded in recognition of the considerable contribution that his shipbuilding and armaments company (Canadian Vickers Company) had made towards the allied war effort. Interestingly, Sir Frederick and his wife also owned a residence on the Côte d'Azur, in Cannes – Villa Viletta. It was to there that the family would frequently repair, hoping that sojourns on the Mediterranean coast would help ease the lingering health problems with which he had had to contend, following his frighteningly close brush with death in 1915. Sir Frederick had been on board RMS Lusitania when, in May of that year, it was infamously sunk by a German U-boat. Miraculously, he survived the ordeal and, in his attention to others in peril at that time, honourably so. But such was the physical and mental toll experienced that he failed to fully recover. He died while convalescing at his villa in November 1921. Aged 55, he was buried in the *Cimetière du Grand Jas* in Cannes. It was three years later that his daughter, Mary Graham, would marry Roy Kennard.

Despite his wayward track record, Roy's marriage flourished. Over the years Mary had tirelessly and affectionately nursed Roy through his various addictions and emotional hang-ups, if such they were. The couple would spend much of their time in the small villa that Roy had arranged to be constructed on the aforementioned plot of land that had once been part of the Eilenroc estate. The villa was to be simply named after that of his wife – 'Villa Mary Graham'. It certainly seemed as though the couple could now look forward to more relaxing and intimate times together, away from the social whirl.

As for Roy's mother, for some time her links with Cap d'Antibes had also been slowly slipping away. Increasingly recluse, she was now firmly entrenched in a personal suite in Claridge's Hotel, London. Those stimulating encounters of yore, with literary figures such as Henry James, Thomas Hardy, H. G. Wells and Arnold Bennett, to name but a notable few, were by now just fading memories. So too were her links with the activist political milieu into which her husband James Carew had introduced her. It was away from the crowd, in her luxurious hotel suite, that she died in April 1928. Helen had led a rich and varied life, and one in which her time in Eilenroc had once figured most prominently.

If her demise struck Roy hard, then, within three years he would suffer an even more devastating and wholly unexpected loss. For in 1931, while sojourning on Cap d'Antibes, his wife Mary contracted lockjaw and died, apparently from a mundane scratch to the leg. She was to be buried alongside her father in the Grand Jas Cemetery in Cannes. Heartbroken, Roy never really recovered. Seeking consolation he turned to his writing. Thus it was, some years after his wife's death, that he was moved to muse on innocently playful times spent at Eilenroc in his younger days. His reflections were emotionally expressed in his *'Farewell to Eilenroc'* (1934). One reviewer would describe it as a *'fragrant and nostalgic account of his childhood in the South of France'*. That same year saw the publication of another book, based this time on his interest in the Middle East and its literary heritage: *'Olympia or How the Secrets of the East were Lost for Ever'*. It is an unusual story in the tradition of the Persian poets, and one that seemed to capture in metaphor, the otherworldliness of his own highly disjointed life. In the first four chapters of the text, a consul snores, dogs devour a woman, the hero consults a witch, and then, to cap it all, there is a tornado and an earthquake. Less well received at this same time, and on another plane altogether, was his collection of intimate poems entitled *'Caresses et blasphèmes'*.[13] Copies of Roy's writings were available in the British Museum Library, but because of their supposedly risqué nature, some were apparently at one point placed on the 'restricted' shelves. These more louche pieces recalled drug-fuelled and hedonistic times past. One reviewer considered such works to be in the style of 'The Yellow Book' – a quarterly periodical, published in the mid 1890s, with a particular emphasis on aestheticism and decadence as literary genres. Coincidentally, given what went on before in the early part of his own life, and indeed that of his mother, the said 'Book', just happens to be referred to in Oscar Wilde's aforementioned novel *'A Picture of Dorian Grey'*.

Come the Second World War, recalcitrant as ever, Roy refused to even consider leaving France. As a result, following the German occupation, he was reputedly interned in a camp at Compiègne as a British citizen. Although not always in the best of health, he survived that particular ordeal and eventually returned to his now more modest home on Cap d'Antibes, from where he presumably looked longingly, and no doubt with mixed feelings, on Eilenroc, his former home. This time, and true to past form, he arrived with a new unnamed partner; one who had apparently served as his clinical nurse during his incarceration. It would seem that his addictions had resurfaced following the death of Mary Graham. But Roy would not enjoy many stays on the cape, for in 1948 he too died, aged 63. He was laid to rest alongside his caring but ill-fated second wife, Mary Graham. Roy apparently left no will, and his home reverted to his first wife. She too died intestate, and rather than the diminished property being inherited by his two sons (by his first marriage), it seemingly went under French law to his wife's sister. It was a complicated ending to a very complicated life. What was to follow was even more so.

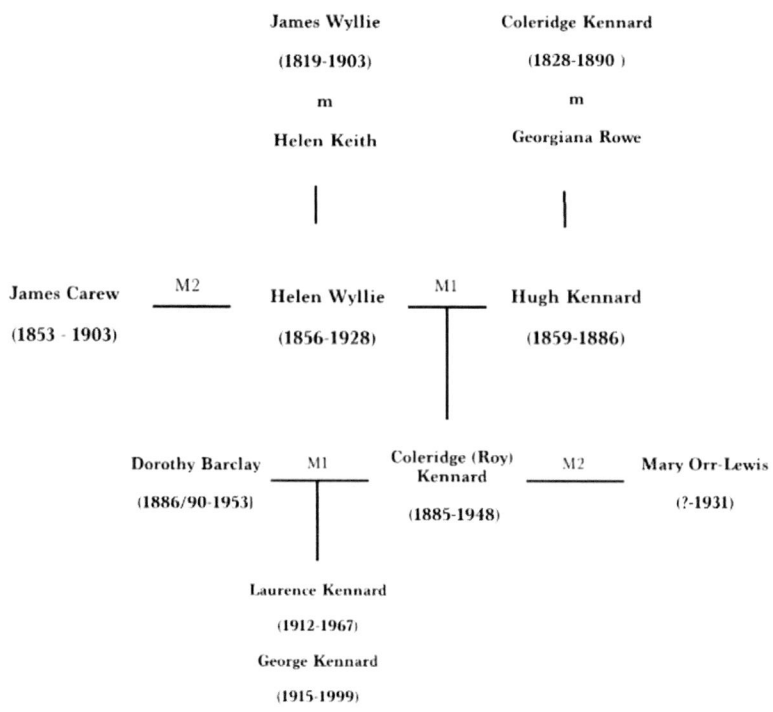

Wyllie and Kennard Family Tree

A Most Extraordinary Affair

In the literature, and in general reporting, there would appear to be considerable confusion and differences of opinion as to who precisely purchased or acquired the Eilenroc estate from the Kennard family, and when and how the transfer of ownership took place. What *is* certain is that two families – the Lebaudys and the Sudreaus – were directly involved. If what went on before was tortuous and tragic, the sequel would prove to be even more so.

The backstory centres initially on one Jacques Lebaudy and his wife (partner/mistress?) – Augustine Léonie Marguerite (née Dellière).[14] Also involved in the unfolding saga was a daughter from the relationship, Jacqueline by name. As to the Sudreaus, father and son, Henri and Jacques, became involved at a later date.

Jacques Lebaudy was the eldest son of Jules Lebaudy (1828-1892) and Amicie Piou (1847-1917). Over the years, the Lebaudy family, and its forebears, had amassed a vast fortune largely from the development of a sugar beet and sugar refining business, but also through investments in a range of asset classes. They included a substantial portfolio of residential and retail properties, as well as a vaudeville theatre in Paris. Astute speculation in stocks and shares added further to the family fortune. On Jules' death, Jacques, together with brothers and a sister, acquired a significant inheritance and a substantial and ongoing flow of disposable income. Further inheritance, following the untimely death of his younger brother Max in 1895, aged 22, added significantly to his already bursting coffers.

Given his wealth and social standing, what seemed very odd to the Parisian *beau monde* was his intimate relationship with a would-be actress of humble background, who hailed from the small village of Lapalud, near Bollène in the Rhône valley. How, it was asked, could a notable member of the Jockey Club, the Yacht Club de France, and the *Société de Steeple-Chase* stoop so low? After all, the lady concerned was clearly not just a passing fancy. Still, Jacques was known to be a law unto himself and more than a little eccentric in his ways. Whatever the occasion he was always dressed in tight fitting garb, with a black cotton umbrella characteristically to hand. Other odd adornments were added, as seen fit. It all depended on how he felt at the time. An out and out maverick, he was hardly what would be expected of a scion of the respected Lebaudy family. However, there was no denying his ability to make money. The only problem was how he would use it. In this regard his decision to build a railway in Africa was particularly bizarre. Others have suggested that, at the same time, he was also considering the establishment of an extensive irrigation system. The project certainly raised eyebrows in the Parisian worlds of business and investment. How could he even dream of such a venture?

From the outset it was obvious that both the French and Spanish authorities would dismiss the project out of hand. It was ludicrous to even think that it might gain approval. Undeterred, Jacques had other ideas. The solution to the impasse was, at least to his way of thinking, quite simple – first establish his own state in the region, an empire indeed, with himself as ruler. In so doing he would be in a position, not only to start work on building the said railway, but also to initiate the process of establishing a benevolent and conservative society, far removed from that prevailing back in left-wing republican France. Thus it was that the inflated idea of becoming 'Emperor Jacques I' of the 'Empire of the Sahara' was born. How he set about the exercise is too complex and outlandish to detail here. But, in brief, it involved his hiring of some sailors and mercenaries, establishing a base in the Canary Islands, from there crossing over to the African shore, making a landing at Cap Juby in southern Morocco, and proclaiming himself overlord. As simple as that! This was in late May, 1903. Jacques was 32. His compliant partner and would-be empress-in-waiting, Augustine, was 30. An

Jacques Lebaudy

imperial household was in the making – *ab initio*. Napoléon and Josephine in another guise.

Having scrambled ashore with his none too merry band, Jacques began by choosing a site for his would-be capital city (to be called Troja) and formally planting his personal flag in the sand. On the spot, he even appointed members of government from within the less than impressive landing party. Looking on at all this were a few bemused tribesmen on camels. Later, some of Jacques' mercenaries were taken captive, and hefty ransoms demanded. It was time to make a hasty retreat, and to head back. By then the whole affair had become a matter of concern and embarrassment to the French and Spanish governments, who could not comprehend what had possessed Lebaudy. Apart from the political sensitivities involved, there was now the pressing practical and political matter as to who would secure the safe release of the captives by paying the ransom demanded. It soon became a matter of wider and rather embarrassing political compass for all concerned. Needless to say, the French and foreign press had a field day. It was an asinine pantomime; of that there could be no doubt.

As for Jacques and Augustine, they would initially seek shelter from the storm in Switzerland. Whilst there, Augustine gave birth to a daughter who would be named Jacqueline. On a birth certificate, completed later in Augustine's home village of Lapalud, it would be stated that her father was 'unknown'. This would later

Jacqueline Lebaudy

prove to be a contentious issue when it came to matters relating to inheritance.

In the meantime Jacques carried on in his quixotic way. He had certainly not relinquished his self-proclaimed imperial title, nor indeed did he feel that he had lost his desert empire. Now in Brussels, he apparently considered taking his case to the International Court at The Hague. In the meantime, with flags flying, he even set up an embassy. Matters became increasingly out of hand, however, when in October 1905 he moved to London, where, without any qualms, he established an Imperial headquarters just off the Strand, in the Savoy Hotel no less. With a sizeable staff at his beck and call, he had

—The Emperor of Sahara's Stampage, Throne, Coinage, and Flag.—

The Emperor of Sahara's Stampage, Throne, Coinage and Flag

further flags, medals, insignia and bank notes designed, an anthem composed, and a throne installed in the midst of the renowned hotel. It is said that an orchestra was also permanently on call, and ordered to play the Saharan national anthem whenever he received visitors deemed to be of some standing. Who they might have been goes unrecorded. With a governmental reshuffle presumably now in order, new Ministers of State were also formally appointed. But no Emperor could be without a court. Ladies of truly noble stock would be hard to come by, but others of lesser status could easily be bought in, as and when the occasion required.

Inevitably, Imperial residence at the Savoy Hotel could not last, and later years would see Jacques and his compliant wife once again on the move. If his vision of a kingdom had been blown away, it did not stop him still thinking about having a territory over which he would be recognized as supreme ruler. With the Principality of Monaco in mind as a model, and just a year after the Saharan fiasco, Jacques apparently approached Prince Nicholas of Montenegro with a view to purchasing a small piece of his territory (around the present-day coastal town of Ulcinj, close to the Albanian border). Unsurprisingly, he received short shrift and yet another pipe dream went up in smoke. But not before he had set about buying up a swathe of residences in the settlement concerned – it did wonders for the local property market. This particular episode is cited here because, ironically, following the outbreak of the Great War, King Nicholas I of Montenegro (as he became in 1910) would eventually find himself living in exile on Cap d'Antibes, and in a residence located just a kilometer or so from Villa Eilenroc! By then, he too had lost a country, but under very different circumstances (see 4). As for Jacques, he had soon had enough of Europe. But the saga does not end there. Indeed, it had only just started.

Having failed to satisfy his imperial aspirations, Jacques Lebaudy decided to pick up sticks and move to America. At first all seemed to go well. A small estate – Phoenix Lodge, located near the settlement of Westbury, Long Island, was purchased as a family home, while Jacques quickly set about making a name for himself as an unusual but wily operator on the floor of the New York Stock Exchange. This he did, but before long his already questionable mental state began to deteriorate, and to an alarming extent. So much so, that he would eventually be sectioned and placed in a local asylum. However, determined as ever, on numerous occasions he absconded and continued to behave bizarrely. The dénouement would not be long in coming.

Thus it was, in January 1919, following another demented and threatening outburst on her husband's part, that his wife, Augustine, ended up killing him. Apparently, in a state of high, demented dudgeon, Jacques had seen fit to burn their home down while Augustine and Jacqueline were inside. There were also reports that he wished to molest his teenage daughter, desperate as he was for a male heir to continue the imperial line. It was all too much. With a gun to hand, Augustine felt she had no option but to shoot her long-term partner. The five shots unleashed would prove to be lethal. It was a desperately sad conclusion to a troubled and very strange relationship. Found to have acted under extreme provocation, Augustine was deemed to be an innocent party by a grand jury and was not indicted. All that now remained was to return to France and to complete the necessary arrangements regarding Jacques' estate. It would prove not to be as straightforward as the Lebaudys had hoped it would be.

It was at this point that a French private detective who happened to have offices in New York, Henri Sudreau by name, offered to help Augustine sort out further legal matters back in France. Later, his son, Roger, would also enter the gilded frame. With the French authorities not recognising the validity of the legal judgments made in America concerning the partitioning of the inheritance, Henri persuaded Augustine that for all concerned there would be much to be gained if they married. Not only that, it would be even better, he suggested, if his son wedded Jacqueline!

Thus in 1922 a father and son would marry a mother and her

daughter. Marguerite was then 49, whilst Jacqueline was just 17. According to some accounts the couples chose to have a joint wedding ceremony in Paris. Apparently, they had tried to do so in Augustine's home village. However, the local priest there reputedly refused to countenance such a heinous arrangement. Finally, there were inevitably those who suggested that the marriages were simply ones of convenience, and in Jacqueline's case that it was a *'mariage blanc'* (unconsummated). No doubt Henri and Roger would not have been concerned with such admonitions. Look what they had fortuitously gained.

At this point it might be asked what, in the interim, had become of Eilenroc. Although the situation is once again unclear, it would appear that the estate came formally into Augustine and Henri Sudreau's hands in 1924. Either this was through a direct purchase of the property on their part, or, more likely, as mentioned above, it was already part of Jacques Lebaudy's estate. If the latter, then how, when and why, he (Jacques) had purchased the property from the Kennards would appear to go unrecorded in the general literature. What is certain, however, is that the Sudreaus must have planned to establish a firm base on Cap d'Antibes, for, according to some sources, Henri became involved in the affairs of the municipality, and even made an attempt to become mayor of the commune. If true, he failed not only in that endeavour, but also in realising plans that he reputably had for the development of the Eilenroc estate. In this particular regard he envisaged dividing up the 11 hectares into plots on which luxury residences would be constructed – a veritable *'cité de grand style'*, as it was to be described in the planning application. Unsurprisingly, the proposal failed to gain the necessary permissions. The heritage value of the site was much too important to suffer dismemberment.

It may have been this, or Henri's sudden death in 1927, that caused the Sudreaus to put the property up for auction, following a French Court's decision that all assets in Jacques' estate in France should be liquidated in settling inheritance issues once and for all. Such confusion apart, what is certain is that in March 1927 Eilenroc was sold, with an asking price having been set at 5 million francs. Others have suggested that the actual figure was much higher than that. Needless to say, the auction attracted considerable international interest – such was the high regard in which the *'domaine'* had long been held, and this despite the fact that over more recent times the residence and its grounds had indubitably not received the care and attention that they demanded and deserved. To bring the whole estate back to life, the new owners would need to be prepared to invest heavily and with sensitivity. Fortunately, they could, and would, do so. The new occupants of Eilenroc were the American entrepreneur Louis Dudley Beaumont and his new wife Hélène.

As for Marguerite, the once would-be Empress of the Sahara, she settled in Paris. It was here that she died in 1950, aged 77. Following her inevitable divorce in 1930, Jacqueline had married a certain René Fréderic Frotté. Details as to her life thereafter are lacking, but it is known that she died in 1974, aged 69. Both she and her mother had most certainly led a roller coaster of a life. They may have done little or nothing as far as Eilenroc was concerned, but they certainly helped to add a most confusing chapter to the biographical history of Eilenroc. Yet another tortuous tragi-comedy had reached its sad end. The same could certainly not be said of the Beaumonts, the next owners of the villa and its grounds. Having acquired Eilenroc, they would add the gloss, glamour and assurance that the residence certainly warranted.

Revival and Renewal

The American retailer, Louis Beaumont (né Schoenberg), together with his brother-in-law, David May and his brothers, Joseph and Moses, established what would become the May Department Stores Company in 1888. The enterprise was immensely successful. In 1912, and by now very wealthy, Louis decided to retire from the business, but would maintain a watching brief as a vice-president.

Rather than remain in America, however, he chose to establish a new residential base for himself in France. When the First World War broke out, rather than return home, he chose to stay and contribute in whatever way he could to the allied war effort. Conscious of the fact that his Germanic family name – Schoenberg – was hardly appropriate under the prevailing circumstances, Louis expeditiously changed it to the nearest French equivalent. From now on he would be styled – Beaumont. Such was his commitment to the cause at this time, which included considerable financial support for a hospital in Paris and for aviators on active service, that in 1920 he was awarded the prestigious French order of merit – *Chevalier de la Légion d'Honneur*.

On a personal front, while in London, Louis had met an aspiring opera singer – Hélène Marguerite Thomas. In 1926 she would become his second wife. His first wife, Flora (née Rothschild), had died in 1891 when just 29 years of age. The couple had had one child – Dudley Cleveland. Distressingly, he too was to die young – aged 25. As to Hélène, she was born in Australia and had moved to Europe to further her career. At the time of their marriage in 1927 she was in her early 30s, while Louis was nearing 70. For Hélène the purchase of Eilenroc so soon after their marriage must have been truly exciting, for the villa would serve as a stunning rendezvous where she could lavishly entertain titled guests, political figures, writers, and celebrities from the world of entertainment, together with sundry representatives of the wider *'beau monde'*. Apart from being a professional singer, Hélène was becoming more and more an accomplished *'salonnière'*.

But before their new residence was deemed to be worthy of the esteemed invitees, it was imperative that Eilenroc itself should be suitably reconfigured and refurbished, and that the grounds should be accorded a radical makeover. For this, only the most highly rated of professionals would be considered. Thus it was that the American architect, William Wells Bosworth, was called upon. Unconstrained, and with money far from being an issue, it was he who added the eye-catching Corinthian columns that would front a tiered staircase. This imposing façade complemented an elegantly decorated interior, adorned with an outstanding collection of French classical furniture, much of it having been acquired from the English Rothschild family. In keeping with the times, however, the house also included highly distinctive modernistic and Art Deco features – including a sumptuous marbled bathroom. It was a facelift of the highest order.

Whilst all this was going on, attention was given to the wholescale rehabilitation of the grounds and gardens. For this, the Beaumonts invited the acclaimed French landscape architect and urban designer – Jacques Gréber to undertake the work. After initial training in Paris, in 1909 he had moved to America where he associated himself with the Beaux-Arts School and the City Beautiful Movement. There, he had gained considerable recognition for his imaginative urban landscaping projects. Following a productive stay of ten years, Gréber left America and returned to France. Soon he would be receiving a whole series of prestigious commissions, an increasing number of which involved the designing of large private estates and gardens. Included in their number was Eilenroc.

In the meantime, Louis would take time out to indulge his longstanding interest in sailing. Like Guy de Maupassant, but on an inordinately grander scale! His new home was ideally located, with the coastal resorts nearby having long attracted owners of eye-catching yachts, many of which would eagerly participate in the numerous regattas and races organized by nautical clubs and associations. Such was Louis's obvious commitment to yachting that he was referred to by many within the fraternity as the '*Commodore*'. But his sporting interests were not confined to sailing; he was also an aficionado of the bourgeoning aviation industry. Again, throughout the Côte d'Azur, resorts were keen to widen their range of entertainments for visitors, including aeronautical displays and races. Clubs were duly formed, one of which was the Aero Club of America in France. Of this Louis was made President.

Louis Dudley Beaumont

Among those who would eventually cross the portals of the revitalized Eilenroc, of particularly high profile were the Duke and Duchess of Windsor. In 1938 they would become close neighbours of the Beaumonts when they (the Windsors) leased Château de la Croë following their controversial marriage (see 5). But there would not be many such encounters since, at around that time, the Beaumonts were preparing to leave for America, following the outbreak of World War Two. But before then, there were many other guests who would add lustre to Eilenroc and its standing as a place of exalted rendezvous. Two couples, who also happened to live nearby, could most certainly count on receiving invitations to Eilenroc.

The first of these was the vastly wealthy businessman Frank Jay Gould and his exuberant and forthright wife, Florence. As noted above, the couple were well known and appreciated locally for having played a key part in transforming the small settlement of nearby Juan-les-Pins into a boisterous modern resort; and in particular one that was to play a key role in the promotion of the summer season on the Côte d'Azur. As it happened, they had come across the area the very same year that the Beaumonts had gained ownership of their prestigious domain. Ironically, Florence Gould and Hélène Beaumont had in their younger days both been trained singers, but with the former having 'functioned' at a much less professional or refined level. Furthermore, it was through their singing that the two hostesses had captured the attention of their husbands-to-be. While the pair seemingly chimed at a social level, it is unlikely that the poised proprietress of Eilenroc would have engaged in the more athletic and flamboyant pursuits that so animated Florence at that time.

The second of the two prominent couples with a local base were the Aga Khan III and his new French wife, formerly Andrée Joséphine Carron, but who now bore the title Princess Aga Khan. The Aga Khan had first met her as the young child of close friends living in Aix-les-Bains (Savoie). Despite the modesty of her background and the disparities in age, she clearly left a lasting impression on the highly influential and very wealthy spiritual leader of the Nizaris (Ismaili Shia Muslims). So much so, that in 1929 the couple were married. It was to be the Aga Khan's third marriage. Shortly after that the couple decided to establish a base for themselves on Cap d'Antibes. Thus it was that they purchased an existing villa, named Taormina. They too would embark upon a lavish wholesale renovation. Located in the heart of Cap d'Antibes, it adjoined the main boulevard (now Boulevard du Cap). Interestingly, for a short period the property had earlier been rented out to Grand Duke Nicholas Nikolaevich, who, living in exile with his wider family, had decided to settle in the locality (see 3). With his new wife romantically in mind, the Aga Khan would name the villa 'Jane Andrée'. A distinctive feature of the greatly enhanced residence was an Art Deco cum neo-Provencal arcade/loggia. The interior was furnished with a blend of classical French pieces and carpets, intermixed with Indian and Persian adornments. The marriage was destined to last for some 14 years.[15]

Besides the Windsors, the Goulds, the Khans and their like, over the years a stream of esteemed guests would attend social evenings and festive gatherings at Eilenroc. Sumptuous candlelight dinners with accompanying firework displays and musical soirées were highlights of the social calendar on the Côte d'Azur. Those attending would surely have appreciated the opportunity to admire the exquisitely revamped interior of the villa itself, and in so doing presumably taken full advantage of the opportunity to admire the carefully selected paintings adorning its walls, and most especially a notable collection by 18th century French masters.[16] For a decade, and even through the years of the Wall Street crash and ensuing economic depression, the Beaumonts managed to maintain their lifestyle at Eilenroc, albeit to a more suitably toned-down degree. But with another World War eventually looming, the couple reluctantly elected to take their leave of Eilenroc, and return to Louis's home in America. Hopefully, with the ending of hostilities, they would soon be returning to Cap d'Antibes.

Hélène would, but not her husband. For, in 1942, Louis died; he was aged 85. Now in her early fifties, but still keen to maintain her engaging lifestyle, Hélène returned to Eilenroc. A degree of normality was established, but only for a short while. Recognising that the villa was far too large for her, but unwilling to simply leave Eilenroc altogether, she arranged for another smaller residence to be built within the grounds. Again, only the best of architects would do. So it was that she called upon one of the most sought-after architects then working on the Côte d'Azur, the American, Barry Dierks. Hélène settled into her new abode, together with her sister, but with Eilenroc simply resting there in a state of suspended animation, and as an all too sentimental reminder of more joyful and elegant times, the decision was later taken to set up a more permanent residence for herself in the Principality of Monaco, where she also owned a luxurious apartment.

But what to do with Eilenroc? Unable to face the prospect of selling the property that had meant so much to her and her husband, Hélène simply mothballed the main residence. It would be many years later, in February 1982, that a socially constructive and most charitable decision was taken as to the future of the villa. She decided not to sell the estate, but to donate it in perpetuity to the citizens of Antibes, with the proviso that a foundation named after her husband should be set up, not only to ensure its safekeeping but also to make use of it in ways that would benefit the municipality. It was an unexpected bequest, and one that would be gratefully acknowledged.

Some six years after having ceded ownership in such munificent a fashion, Hélène Beaumont died at the age of 94. The auction of her extensive possessions, which was organised by Sotheby's, was a three day affair. The catalogue for the sale was entitled: *'Succession de Mme Hélène Beaumont: provenant de la Villa Eilenroc au Cap d'Antibes'*. Held in Geneva in 1992, a much–publicised and sought-after highlight among a vast array of outstanding items was the sale of a stupendous diamond and emerald necklace in Art-Deco style. The necklace alone was sold for just over 3 million euros.

Eilenroc

Villa Eilenroc: Family Sagas

Diligently cared for by the municipality, with its interior being refurbished and its ground embellished, Eilenroc would continue to receive visitors, but now of a much wider cohort. It was a venue that would attract both locals and visitors from afar. Some would leisurely wander the grounds, which would later include a special olive grove, a rose garden and eco-museum; others would attend concerts or as delegates to conferences and reunions. Many more would skirt the grounds, and take in the coves and grottoes of the *'Baie des Milliardaires'*, as they made their way along the highly popular *'Sentier du Littoral'*.

Eilenroc would once again come alive and, in so doing, justify its earlier designation as *'la perle de la Côte d'Azur'*. Or, as some would have it: *'Merveille des Merveilles'*. James Wyllie, in particular, would have been pleased with the edifying ending to what was a long and, at times, unbelievably tumultuous series of family sagas.

Eilenroc: Viewed from Sentier du Littoral

3
Villa Soleil, Grand Hôtel du Cap and Château des Enfants

Introduction

In his guide to the Côte d'Azur, Stéphen Liégeard expressed surprise when, while assiduously gathering information on the locality, he came across a rather down-at-heel hotel set on an otherwise outstanding site on the very tip of Cap d'Antibes, looking out as it did over the wide and all-embracing *'Baie de Golfe Juan'*. In the foreground lay the verdant islands of *Île Sainte-Marguerite* and *Île Saint-Honorat*, whilst in the far distance the serrated outline of the *Massif de l'Esterel* defined the horizon. As to the hotel itself, which he referred to as Hôtel Soleil, it had clearly failed to do justice to its setting. It had certainly seen better days. The matter caused Liégeard to linger awhile, and to muse on how this sorry state of affairs might somehow be redressed. He described the hotel as *'a vast quadrilateral that, in its silence, recalled the castle of Sleeping Beauty'*. Surely, he reflected, something could be done to animate the place, welcoming, in particular, a flow of discerning visitors from northern climes. After all, elsewhere along the coast, and over a goodly number of years, similar, and less well situated, establishments had successfully done so. With its imposing facade, its courtly entrance and its gardens stretching down to the sea via a grand walkway there was indeed much still to admire. It may now have looked a little the worse for wear, but the basics were surely in place.

In Liégeard's view, all that was needed was someone with the will and the resources to invest. If not, then perhaps the hotel should resign itself to becoming a school, a hospice or even a health centre. Were none of these options to prove a viable proposition, then perhaps in the end it would be down to some noble Lord who would indulge a fantasy and bring some life back to the moribund residence. A kiss of life from a 'Prince Charming' no less. Should such a guardian angel not materialize, then the building would surely become a weed-ridden stone corpse engulfed by wild mallows and nettles. As it was to turn out, Liégeard's worse case scenario would not come to pass. Indeed, very soon after his fleeting encounter, someone with the much-needed entrepreneurial drive and imagination would appear on the scene. With encouragement from others, and with timely financial backing, a young hotelier was prepared to take on the challenge. What, under his auspices, would soon become the more than acceptable Grand Hôtel du Cap, would in the long term transform itself into the highly prestigious Hotel du Cap–Eden-Roc (sic) of international renown. It is a story of revival and renewal.

Background

The hotel, over which Liégeard had cast his mournful and questioning eye, first emerged, albeit in embryo form, as a result of the energising and enterprising efforts of the elegantly named Jean Hippolyte Auguste Delaunay de Villemessant – publisher since 1854 of the newspaper '*Le Figaro*'. From the outset his intention was to establish a residential complex that would serve as a peaceful and healthy retreat for weary and infirm '*gens de lettres*'. Artistic souls of various types (writers, musicians, artists etc.), he believed, were prone to suffer from a Pandora's box of ailments, of which:

Villa Soleil, Grand Hôtel du Cap and Château des Enfants

'la phtisie, l'hypertrophie du coeur, l'épuisement prématuré, affections qui exigent un traitement difficile et coûteux, dont l'abstention de plaisirs tumultueux et l'éloignement de Paris sont une des premières conditions'.

[consumption, enlargement of the heart, premature exhaustion, ailments that require difficult and costly treatment, including abstention from tumultuous pleasures and a distancing from Paris are some of the first conditions.]

The reference to the beneficial impact of being as far away as possible from Paris, and its excessive pleasures, was pointed. Much safer, he believed, if such sensitive souls were tucked well away from the bright and dissipating lights of the capital, and in a place where, with like-minded brethren, they might recover their strength and mental equilibrium. What better location than on a soothing southern shore to re-activate creative juices? However, it has to be said that Villemessant's vision was not solely welfare-based, for his plan was just part of a broader speculation in property development that apparently envisaged access to a casino and other '*divertissements*', whatever they may have been. So much for the retreat from Paris! To help realise his plan, a consortium was duly formed with financial backing from hopeful investors.

In his posthumously published '*Souvenirs Littéraires*', the writer/journalist Felix Duquesnel tells of Villemessant's first visit to Cap d'Antibes in the early 1860s.[1] He was apparently on his way to Monte Carlo in the company of the acclaimed playwright, Adolphe d'Ennery. Both had an eye for development opportunities and were more than impressed with the locality. It was, in their view, a charming, quiet promontory, and one that had clearly been by-passed, disregarded or simply gone unnoticed by '*Tout-Paris*'. A key next step, and one that in the long run would prove crucial, was the purchase of a suitable plot of land on the southern periphery of Cap d'Antibes. To finance the operation, Villemessant linked up with a family of Russian property developers – Count Fersen and his brother–in-law Alexis de Plestcheyeff, plus other investors. A prominent site was quickly located, just to the west of where Villa Eilenroc would soon be established. It was here in 1869 that Villemessant hoped to realise his high-minded vision. He even accorded the place a name. Rather unimaginatively for a man of letters, it was to be called Villa Soleil and was to be constructed in the style referred to as Napoleon III. It would be a solidly-built and elegant structure, and its siting would gain significantly from a *'Grande Allée'* that would lead, in equally imperial fashion, down to the rock-fronted seashore. This wide boulevard would become a defining feature, and owed its existence to Count Fersen.

By this time, however, Villemessant suddenly, and inexplicably, lost interest in the whole enterprise. He simply packed his bags and took himself off, first to Nice, and then to the Principality of Monaco. There, luxuriously housed and suitably recompensed by those with vested interests in the place, he set about lauding the attractions of his new home in *Le Figaro*, both as a venue for entertainment and as an unmissable investment opportunity. Why his noble endeavour in aid of 'men of letters' on Cap d'Antibes foundered it is difficult to say. Funding issues undoubtedly played their part. Still, with roulette wheels now spinning in the background, it was most certainly something of a moral volte-face on his part. But then, perhaps it was to be expected, for Villemessant had led a tumultuous life himself, bankruptcies and even jail being part of his curriculum vitae. However, it was in Monaco in 1879 that he would end his days.

As to his soulmate, the dramatist Adolphe d'Ennery, who had accompanied him on their first visit to Cap d'Antibes, he too had eventually pulled out of the main venture. Nevertheless, so taken was he with the area that, in 1865, he had set about having a most elegant villa constructed for himself just a short distance from the would-be Villa Soleil – it was to be called *'Les Chênes Verts'*. There he would receive many well-known figures from the world of the arts, most of whom were lauded in Parisian society. Included among them was the writer Jules Verne. In the villa the pair collaborated

Hippolyte Villemessant   Adolphe d'Ennery

on a number of projects including, most famously, adaptations for the stage of Verne's novels – '*Le Tour du Monde en 80 Jours*' ('Around the World in Eighty Days') in 1874 and '*Michel Strogoff*' (1876).

Whilst Villemessant failed to follow through on his '*pensée très humanitaire*', as Liégeard graciously referred to it, others were to follow who saw far greater potential in the development of a fully commercial hotel on the site. Thus it was, that, with a reconstituted *Compagnie du Cap d'Antibes* overseeing matters, the Villa Soleil would reincarnate itself as the Hôtel Soleil. The hotel itself was officially launched on Saturday, 26 February 1870. The opening celebrations were reportedly sumptuous in the extreme, and attended by the cosmopolitan cream of Riviera society.

The timing of the inauguration could not have been more unfortunate, for within five months, France was at war with Prussia. The titled and leisured classes who might have been drawn to the place no longer thought of sojourning on the Mediterranean coast – at least not in any great numbers – and the hotel venture seemed doomed from the outset. The widespread economic depression

Hôtel Soleil 1870 – Inauguration

that ensued, following the ending of hostilities, certainly did not help matters. In 1876 the *Compagnie du Cap d'Antibes* that had attempted to guide the hotel through to calmer waters was forced into liquidation. Alexis de Plestcheyeff, who had remained committed to the venture following Count Fersen's death from tuberculosis in 1865, was one of those who would suffer losses. Despite efforts to do so, it proved impossible to find a buyer for many years. Indeed it was not until 1884 that another consortium of investors stepped in to try and retrieve the situation. It was while strenuous, but seemingly unavailing, efforts were being made by the new owners to turn the ship around that Stéphen Liégeard cast eyes on the structure. His soon to be published observations would have done little to help market the place.

It was very shortly after Liégeard's passing encounter that fortune would smile on the hotel venture. For in 1887 the young hotelier, Antoine Sella, appeared on the scene. He came from an enterprising extended family, but had himself been orphaned at the age of 6. The family had its main roots in Biella, a small settlement located on the southern fringes of the Alps, and some 80 kilometres to the northeast of Turin. Keen to establish a career for himself in hotel management, and with financial support from kith and kin, he gained much from running a small spa hotel in the nearby settlement of Andorno. It focussed upon hydrotherapy, and really only functioned during the months of summer. Before long his thoughts turned to the management of a hotel on the shores of the Mediterranean, where since the 1830s members of European high society had increasingly been gathering for long winter sojourns. The prospect of turning around a struggling venture clearly appealed to him, for in 1887 Sella took up the offer to manage the ailing Hôtel Soleil. Just two years later it would become the Grand Hôtel du Cap. Working initially on commission, and within a tight budget, he embarked upon a modest restructuring of the interior. Fortunately, he was energetic, talented, driven and full of ideas. When he first took over the reins, it is said that there were just two old English ladies in residence, each paying a measly 12 francs a day for their residence. Worryingly for Sella and the forty or so staff, it looked at first as though it would be extremely difficult to attract a sufficient flow of visitors to make the whole enterprise a going concern. No doubt a little nervously, just over a year after taking up managerial control, he arranged a formal opening of the revamped hotel. Word soon spread and within a year or so occupation levels were of a surprisingly high order.

 A notable initiative in these early days was the establishment of a magnificently sited teahouse, and later a small restaurant, on the rocky coastal frontage. A further development, that would become a truly iconic feature of the hotel, was the creation of a seawater plunge pool. It was blasted out of the basalt rock and would become a favoured and frolicsome meeting point for guests.

At the time, the hotel management also actively encouraged 'excursionists' paying visits to Cap d'Antibes, to call in and sample all that it had to offer. Of those taking up the opportunity, there would be many who, arriving by carriage, and indeed by bicycle, came specifically to wander the nearby grounds of James Wyllie's Villa Eilenroc. But increasingly it was not just passing guests who would frequent the hotel and make use of its facilities. More and more would stay on a regular basis, and look forward to savouring both its increasingly *'haute cuisine'* and its relaxed and select atmosphere. Of these, many owned villas elsewhere along the coast. Early habitués included the hapless Grand Duke Fredrick Francis III of Mecklenburg-Schwerin and his Russian wife, Grand Duchess Anastasia Mikhailovna. They spent much of the year at their home in Cannes – Villa Wenden, but would often take the opportunity to dine at the hotel and to admire its exquisite setting. Another regular visitor was James Gordon Bennett Junior. Extremely wealthy, he had taken over the New York Herald from his father, and had later established international editions of the paper. Although based in Paris, he too owned a residence along the coast in Beaulieu-sur-Mer. Not only that, he had a vested financial interest in *'La Réserve de Beaulieu'*; a highly rated hotel and restaurant in the small but exclusive resort. He would most certainly not have frequented Sella's establishment were it not of the highest standard. Perhaps he would even learn something. Indeed, more than suitably impressed, Bennett would later arrange for his sister and a large circle of her friends to take up residence there for a long stay. By then, the Grand Hôtel du Cap had succeeded in fashioning an international reputation for itself, and was now receiving more and more guests who would take up residence during the winter season.

In a travel guide to the Rivieras, published in 1897, Augustus Hare, not an easy critic to please at the best of times, said of the hotel that it was *'beautifully situated in large grounds of its own'*, and had '*an exquisite view towards Golfe Juan and Cannes*'. Furthermore, it was '*admirably managed*' and '*one of the quietest and best winter residences on the Riviera for invalids who are not seriously ill*'. Sella could not have asked for more.

Positive reviews and commendatory words of mouth may have been accumulating, but Sella appreciated the need not to rest on his laurels. It was all too apparent that, as elsewhere along the coast, both 'palace' and 'grand' hotels were rapidly re-equipping themselves to ever-higher levels, and that competition would be commensurately intense. A radical modernization was a must. But for that, more investment would have to be sourced. Without it, it would simply not be possible to introduce such prerequisites as electric lighting, lifts, central heating, en-suite bathrooms and even running water throughout.

The dilemma for Sella was that while, over the years, he had steadily acquired more shares in the hotel, there seemed little

Antoine Sella and Lord Onslow

prospect of his gaining outright control. In his view, only if he did so would he feel able to expedite the necessary developments and face the growing competition head on. As the sole proprietor he would find it easier to seek out the necessary finance to undertake the improvements in facilities and services that were now so plainly demanded. Fortuitously, a white knight would surface in the form of a wealthy and frequent guest at the hotel. It is said that, out of the blue, when Sella was expounding on his hopes and dreams, a regular and appreciative guest – Lord William Hillier Onslow, 4th Earl of Onslow,[2] stated that he would make available the funds needed to secure the control the hotelier needed. The year was 1903, and the sum dispensed 500,000 francs. Lord Onslow apparently left the issue of repayment open for discussion at a later date. It was a serendipitous vote of confidence. Liégeard's noble Lord had finally arrived! The world was now Sella's oyster.

Lord Onslow and his wife, Florence, continued to be honoured

Grand Hôtel du Cap

Villa Soleil, Grand Hôtel du Cap and Château des Enfants

Pavilion Eden-Roc and Rock Pool

guests at the hotel, and were able to appreciate the quality of many of the improvements that were being made to the main building and its grounds. Sadly, however, Lord Onslow himself would not be there to witness the grand opening in 1914 of the expanded rock pool at the water's edge, or to dine in the upmarket restaurant, which would replace the former facilities. He had passed away some three years earlier. Such was the distinctiveness of this latter complex, set as it was on the cliff edge and at the end of the *'Grande Allée'*, that Sella deemed it worthy of a separate designation. Henceforth, it would be referred to as the 'Pavilion Eden-Roc'.

The future certainly looked promising. But then, in no time at all, the situation changed dramatically. History was about to repeat itself. In 1870 it was the outbreak of the Franco-Prussian War; now it was the advent of the First World War. It meant that for the time being all of Sella's plans would have to be put on hold. Like many other hotel owners and managers across the region, he had to make ready for the conversion of his prized possession into a sanatorium, and a place for rest and recuperation for those who had served in the various zones of military conflict. Over the following six years, the management of the Grand Hôtel du Cap was in the hands of the American Red Cross. For those nurses and doctors mentally scarred in the zones of conflict, there could not have been a more comforting milieu in which to seek recovery.

Following the ending of hostilities, every effort was made to ensure that the hotel was reinstated to its former glory. However, simply resting on past laurels was not an option. Further investment was a *'sine qua non'*. At the time it was hoped that the winter season would eventually re-establish itself. It did, but very slowly and very tentatively. Then, almost out of the blue, and as previously described (see 1), came the emergence of summer tourism. Sella was quick to recognise the opportunities that opened up for the hospitality sector at large and made every effort to take full advantage of them.

Amidst the exuberance of those heady times, Sella soon found himself catering for a whole array of guests from increasingly varied walks of life. The titled and the privileged (Old Money) would still arrive, although there were far fewer of them about. Joining them now, and increasingly in their stead, were celebrities of the emerging film industry, writers, composers, choreographers and dancers, as well as prominent artists from all corners of the world. Political figures of eminence also called in (e.g. the Kennedys), as indeed did those who were then making fortunes in finance and industry. The realm of fashion and haute couture was also well represented. What better place to display one's wares? Given the changing tastes and associated lifestyles, Sella saw benefits in opening up private cabins called *'cabanas'*, discreetly set apart and dispersed around the hotel grounds amidst fragrant pine groves. They quickly became a distinctive and defining feature of the hotel's profile.

But then came the 1929 stock-market crashes and the global Depression that followed. By this time the highly respected Antoine Sella had presumably seen enough. He died in 1931, and the management of the hotel was now firmly in the hands of his son, André. He it was who would now have to address the task of steering the ship through even more choppy waters. But having worked alongside his father for so long, he was more than ready to face the challenges that now lay ahead. Improvements would continue to be made, and high standards would continue to be assured. Until, that is, he too decided to call it a day. No doubt, in taking his leave, he looked back on how much creative energy he, and in particular his esteemed father, had invested in their internationally renowned hotel. Antoine had passed away before it was published, but he, more than anyone, would surely have appreciated Scott Fitzgerald's depiction of *'Hôtel des Étrangers'* in his novel *'Tender is the Night'*.

Grand Hôtel du Cap

'On the pleasant shore of the French Riviera, about half way between Marseilles and the Italian border, stands a large, proud, rose-colored hotel. Deferential palms cool its flushed façade, and before it stretches a short dazzling beach. Lately it has become a summer resort of notable and fashionable people; a decade ago it was almost deserted after its English clientele went north in April. Now, many bungalows cluster near it, but when this story begins only the cupolas of a dozen old villas rotted like water lilies among the massed pines between Gausse's Hôtel des Étrangers and Cannes, five miles away. The hotel and its bright tan prayer rug of a beach were one'.

It was the Grand Hôtel du Cap in all but name. Fitzgerald knew it well, as did so many others of that 'Lost Generation'.

Villa Soleil, Grand Hôtel du Cap and Château des Enfants

Hôtel du Cap

Le Château des Enfants: Dance and Calisthenics

In highlighting some of the chance events and formative encounters that ultimately helped to contribute to the emerging vogue for summer tourism on the Côte d'Azur, reference is worth making to the invitation extended by the Sellas to a group of young dancers, gymnasts and artists who, in August 1923, were attending a training and study school, then being held at an adjoining villa. One that was eventually to be oddly-named Château des Enfants. The invitation was for those concerned, mainly a group of young (and youngish) ladies, to make use of the grounds of the Grand Hôtel du Cap, and in particular its swimming pool set into the coastal rocks just below the recently remodeled complex known as Eden Roc. Their graceful and animated presence in mid-summer would surely help to further promote and publicise the hotel. Suitably choreographed and professionally photographed, for a very short time at least it would prove to do so. Alluring pictures advertising the hotel would soon be appearing in prestigious magazines (e.g. Vogue, Tatler and The Graphic) and in marketing brochures dispatched throughout Europe and America. The Grand

119

Hôtel du Cap, they excitedly announced, was more than ready to receive youthful, fun-loving and physically inclined visitors. On the social front, times were rapidly changing. But it was not just the group of dancers *per se* who would add to the animated social scene. Associating with them, albeit fleetingly, was a medley of vibrant characters. They would include two key founding figures, together with a number of artists and ideologues of strong leftist persuasion.

As to Château des Enfants itself, it had only recently come into the possession of a wealthy philanthropist, educationalist and social activist – George Davison. Over a number of years, he had served as patron and sponsor to a number of such summer schools. The brainchild of a professional dancer and well-being guru – Margaret Morris – they had previously been held in various parts of Britain and elsewhere in northern France where inclement and unreliable weather had always been a vexatious problem. Now, with Davison having decided to relocate to the Riviera, and his willingness to continue serving as a figurehead, Morris eagerly seized upon the opportunity to run her courses on the shores of the Mediterranean. The initiative would prove to be a considerable success. So much so, that the Margaret Morris Summer Schools – as they were called – would continue to be held over a number of years to come. Antoine Sella and his son André were more than keen to continue the association. For a while at least it could only be good for business, by adding a distinctive degree of piquancy. A minor phase in the long history of the hotel it may have been, but the story is worthy of elaboration – if only because of the characters involved.

George Davison and the Margaret Morris Summer Schools

George Davison was born in 1855 in Kirkley, a small coastal settlement located close to the port of Lowestoft in the county of Suffolk. His father was a carpenter and shipwright, while his mother sought to boost the family income by taking in boarders. They were hard workers. George proved to be equally assiduous and, despite his humble background, eventually qualified sufficiently to serve as a clerk within the civil service. Resident in London, he courted and then married Susanna Potter. In 1884 she gave birth to a son, Ronald, followed in 1889 by a daughter, Ruby. It was around this time that George began to take a serious interest in photography. Such was his commitment and aptitude that he soon became an influential member of a group of photographers whose emphasis was on capturing impressionistic images. In this latter regard, his celebrated print entitled 'An Old Farmstead' (later retitled 'The Onion Field') excited considerable debate. Following wider disputes within the profession, George subsequently became a leading light in the setting up of an avant-garde organization to be called the 'Linked Ring'. One of its central remits was to encourage and promote so-called 'artistic' photography.

In 1889, not long after the establishment of this breakaway group, Davison was approached by George Eastman, the American owner of the 'Eastman Photographic Materials Company' with a view to his becoming a manager of its European affairs. Displaying organizational flair, and exhibiting a deep personal commitment to the promotion of photography and associated technological developments (cameras and film), within a year or two George was appointed 'managing director'. The company flourished globally, and would soon change its name to 'Eastman Kodak'. During the years that he remained in post, Davison astutely amassed a substantial portfolio of share options. As a consequence he became extremely wealthy.

Over the years to come, George nurtured wider cultural interests, whilst at the same time being drawn to social causes and radical thinking. Soon he was giving financial and moral support to organizations that sought to improve the well-being of deprived families and to broaden access to educational opportunities for workers. Across the country, further support was given to the purchase of meeting places for workers associations, the distribution of study materials and the organization of appropriate lectures. The provision of holidays and trips away for children was also high on his philanthropic agenda. More than that, he even felt moved to adopt a number of abandoned children – reputedly nine in all. Perhaps not surprisingly, these 'extra-mural' activities became a cause of some concern within the Kodak Company, where they were deemed to be a little too radical, and not appropriate for its image.[3] Appreciating the situation, and knowing where his heart now lay, in 1912 George resigned his exalted position, and looked forward to committing himself more fully to his wider interests. True to form, the very year that he handed in his notice, he vested funds in a new, but what would turn out to be a short-lived magazine, that bore the title – 'The Anarchist'. By now there were even those who, misguidedly, referred to him as an eccentric 'communist'.

Perhaps sensing that he would soon be severing professional ties with Kodak, George had already progressed his dream of establishing a second home to which he and his family could repair, well away from London. He could not have chosen a more remote spot – Harlech on the stormy far west coast of Wales. With a prominent site purchased, he commissioned the architect George Walton – a friend of Charles Rennie Mackintosh, to draw up plans for a substantial mansion. Named 'Wern Fawr' in Welsh ('Great Alder' in English), it would soon become a meeting place for eclectic gatherings of political activists, artists, singers, musicians and assorted intellectuals. By this time, 1913, George had parted from his first wife, and would later marry Florence Austin-Jones, whom he had initially invited to serve as a housekeeper at what would evolve into a home-cum-study centre.

While based in London, George had, over the years, often attended and supported theatrical and educational classes organized by Margaret Morris.[4] Held in the evenings they combined dance and theatrical sessions with music, calisthenics, and lectures on self-improvement and well-being. Wider political issues would also be debated, with noted radical speakers often leading discussions. Parts of this package of activities would eventually be formalized into a personal development programme known as the *'Margaret Morris Movement'*. Beyond the series of evening classes, the movement would also be delivered through annual Summer Schools. With many of the physical activities being based out of doors, and with coastal locations being favoured, it was inevitable that Morris would later take advantage of an invitation from Davison to hold such a school in Harlech, with access being assured to his home, especially for evening concerts, and when the weather took a turn for the worse, as it frequently did.

In the end, the inclemency of the weather was to become a factor in encouraging George to seriously rethink his move to West Wales. He still owned a substantial property in London to which he could easily return, but with the health of his two-year old daughter, Doreen, an increasing cause of concern, and feeling increasingly frail himself, thought was eventually given to a further relocation. In 1921, and responding to a commendation from Margaret Morris's partner, the highly-regarded Scottish artist, John Duncan Fergusson ('Fergus'), Davison decided to move abroad, and in particular to the then nascent resort of Juan-les-Pins. Fergus spoke effusively of the place, having over the years spent time in the locality, honing his artistic skills.

George was aged 67 when he decided to head south in search of a more salubrious clime. Securing a residence proved to be straightforward. Set close to the shore and named Villa Gotte, it looked out over the Baie de Golfe-Juan. For the family it was another world. More than that, by chance, they were also arriving at the resort just as it was about to experience a period of unprecedented growth and popularity. The move certainly proved beneficial on the health front, but shortly after having settled in, it became evident that despite its attractive location, Villa Gotte itself did not satisfy all of the family's needs. Located in close proximity to the rather shabby municipal casino did not help matters either. A larger and more secluded place, and one with access to a private beach would be ideal. But did such a property exist locally? Coincidentally, in late December of that very year, Margaret Morris and Fergus were invited to join the family for the Xmas festivities. Later, in her autobiography, Margaret would fondly recall: *'I remember that we had Christmas dinner out of doors in the sun'*. It would seem that with the conversation turning to the issue of another property, Fergus mentioned a neglected and unfinished villa on the tip of Cap d'Antibes; one that he had come across many years earlier when he was searching out sites at which to set up his easel. Admittedly it was some time ago, but perhaps it was available for purchase – it was worth checking out.

The property that Fergusson had espied in 1912 was set in grounds that had long ago been in the ownership of the would-be property developer, James Close. It will be recalled that his wider plans for the development of Cap d'Antibes failed to materialize

George Davison

Margaret Morris

because of his untimely death. As to the plot of land itself, it abutted the site on which Hippolyte de Villemessant had hoped to establish Villa Soleil – his convalescent home for debilitated writers. It would appear that, following Close's demise, the domain was eventually divided into two separate tracts. On one, Villa Hier would eventually be constructed (see 5). The other was later to be purchased by King Leopold II of Belgium. At the time he already owned large tracts of land on Cap Ferrat, to say nothing of the Belgian Congo. Although his eminence embarked upon the construction of a villa, the project was not followed through to completion. It has been suggested that Leopold had intended the place to be for his young lover at that time, Cléo de Mérode. As it happened, she too was a professional ballet dancer and performed at venues around the world. More than that, such were her sultry looks, captivating eyes and fulsome hairstyle that she was much sought-after by eager painters and photographers.

Whether or not it was because her relationship with Leopold

Summer School Participants

André Sella Joins In

eventually foundered that the proposed villa was not completed is uncertain. Bizarrely, in her autobiography, Margaret Morris claimed that it was because of a dispute with the local authorities concerning the future height of the proposed villa. In particular, that it would cut the beam emanating from the lighthouse on the Plateau de la Garoupe. Given its location, this seems a little far-fetched. What is beyond doubt, however, is that, when Davison and his guests looked around the place, they were apparently faced with a single storey building, without a proper roof and with trees sprouting 'in the stately rooms'. According to Morris, the windows were 'immensely high, about 12 feet, and the building itself was about 200 feet long, divided into six or seven large rooms'. In the end, the site and the situation were what really mattered. Set among pines and with access to a secluded and private beach, it clearly had potential. Without delay, in 1922, just a year after having moved into Villa Gotte, Davison became the owner of the property and arranged for plans to be drawn up. Soon he and his family would once again be on the move. Appropriately enough, given his longstanding concern for the welfare of children, Davison chose to name their new home 'Château des Enfants'.

Interestingly, the relocation took place in the very year that Cole Porter would be renting nearby Château de la Garoupe for the second time. Not only that, the wealthy and influential American family – the Murphys – would also be based at the Grand Hôtel du Cap whilst they too were seeking out a home for themselves – a place that they would eventually call Villa America.

Given her experiences holding summer schools in places where the weather seldom favoured outdoor activities, it was hardly surprising that Margaret Morris would leap at the offer George Davison made concerning the possibility of holding her next venture on Cap d'Antibes. Doubtless his new residence was hardly in a fit state to take in boarders, but by the summer of 1923 it could at least be used for lectures and parties. This was hardly a problem, for there were plenty of places close by where the necessary accommodation could be secured. The Hôtel Beau Site proved to be especially suitable, and reasonably priced. There was an issue concerning the cost of travel for those attending the school from Britain, but Morris was keen to point out that a ticket from London to Antibes was available at £7 and 10 shillings – third class! In her autobiography, she also makes the revealing comment that taking on local staff to assist with the running of the two-week course would not be a problem since, as she put it, 'everyone on the coast' was 'unemployed in the summer'. Possibly so, but it would not be for long. Times and seasons were changing fast.

The first summer school on Cap d'Antibes was held in 1923. Margaret organized rhythmic dance and gymnastics classes with plastic posing in diaphanous Greek tunics. Overseeing the programme was another noted dancer, Loïs Hutton. She, together with her partner, the French dancer Hélène Vanel, would later set up their own small theatre in the hill village of Saint Paul de Vence. Art classes, with Fergusson to the fore, added further variety. Needless to say, he would take full advantage of the time spent in the area to add to his own *oeuvres*, a goodly number of which refer specifically in their titles to Eden Roc (sic) and Château des Enfants. In keeping with the times, many of his colourful and sometimes lustful, paintings and drawings would be of beaches and bathers, with palms and pines underlining the hedonistic tropicality of the place.[5] Whilst a willing participant in the summer school, Fergus would no doubt have been mindful of the fact that, back home in Scotland, his very first solo exhibition had just opened in Edinburgh. He had come a long way since he first established himself in his Paris studio, a decade or so earlier.

Among the guests at the Grand Hôtel du Cap, when one of the summer schools was being held, were Pablo Picasso and his Russian wife, the former ballet dancer, Olga Khokhlova. They had been invited to join the Murphys. Picasso may not have been overly impressed with the dancing, but Margaret Morris later claimed that she herself had been befriended by the couple and had even joined them on a boat trip out to the nearby Îles de Lérins. Margaret was clearly unimpressed with Olga, writing in her autobiography that:

> 'Picasso's first wife was a ballet dancer and was only interested in the pearls and diamonds Picasso had given her, so my main occupation on these trips to the islands was to 'hold on to her jewels' (sic) while she bathed. I felt like throwing them into the sea'.

If true, they were harsh words regarding a fellow professional dancer, and one who had, until relatively recently, graced Diaghilev's company – the *'Ballets Russes'*. Picasso was a little more measured when voicing his opinion on the 20 or so ladies attending the summer school, as they disported themselves around the pool and in the grounds of the hotel. Later, he apparently told art critic Clive Bell that *'all of them swam divinely, but could not dance at all'*. Maybe so, but that did not stop Picasso from taking advantage of the opportunity to compile sketches of them as they ornamented neighbouring beaches.

While there, Picasso was certainly pleased to come across Fergus, whom he warmly greeted as *'mon vieux copain'*. They had often crossed each other's paths back in bohemian Paris. No doubt with tongue firmly in cheek, Fergus expressed his amused surprise at seeing Picasso in such luxurious surroundings. He was duly informed that while he (Picasso) disliked the place intensely, it suited his aging mother, Dona Maria, who was with him at that time.[6]

The 1923 summer school proved to be a major success. So much so that another was arranged for the following year. Once again Antoine Sella was keen to maintain the link, even to the extent of making some cottages available for the girls. Reflecting on that particular time, Morris noted:

'We all had to work very hard, but we enjoyed every minute, giving performances at night in the hotel grounds. Mr Sella took endless trouble, installing raised seating and hiding spotlights in the trees, thus enabling us to achieve some wonderful effects. The shows were well advertised, and we got an audience from all along the coast. When the French fleet was at Juan-les-Pins, Mr Sella gave dances and invited the naval officers to them, so my girls had a gay time. Some of them remember the number of ice-creams they consumed on these occasions, for Mr Sella was a generous provider.'

Equally accommodating was Davison. Not only did he continue to support the summer school initiative, he also welcomed to his home many who happened to be staying in the area. One interesting visitor who was invited to join Xmas celebrations at Château des Enfants was the gifted, prolific, and highly charismatic American

Max Eastman

writer, poet and radical political commentator – Max Eastman.[7] On the ideological front he and George Davison would surely have had much to talk about. Not least, the political, economic and social state of play in Bolshevik Russia, from where Eastman had only just returned.

Whilst in Russia, Max had committed himself to learning the language, and had thereby managed to cultivate personal contacts with key players. This was made that much easier since he was known by the Russian authorities to have reported favourably on the ideals of the Revolution. Significantly, he had even managed to establish a reasonably close personal relationship with Leon Trotsky, to the extent that he was given permission to write an authorized biography.[8] Having travelled widely around Russia, Max was able to offer a first-hand assessment of the impact that the implementation of a new socio-economic and political order was having on everyday life. He was still there, in the resort of Sochi on the Black Sea, when in January 1924 he heard of Lenin's death. Sochi would figure later, but in a very different context (see 5). In this case it would not be Lenin, but Vladimir Vladimirovich Putin who would be to the fore, albeit very cursorily. No doubt, both Davison and Eastman would have looked quizzically on the Romanov exiles who had, or were about to, take up residence nearby.

With political matters now hanging in the balance, and with Stalin lurking ominously in the wings, Max decided it was an opportune time to take his leave of what was now the Union of Soviet Socialist Republics. His devoted Russian partner at the time, Eliena (Elena) Kyrlenco, was desperate to accompany him out of the country, but acquiring a passport proved to be problematical. In the end, the only solution to the impasse was to marry. It was not a prospect that the ever-charming Max would have chosen, since he was known to be an inveterate womanizer, and abhorred the idea of such a singular commitment as marriage. But, under the circumstances, needs must.[9] Not that Eliena was unaware of Max's proclivities; his 'seizures' as she put it. But she was prepared to live with 'them'. Such personal matters apart, now armed with the necessary documentation, the couple were able to make their way out of an increasingly vindictive political régime. England would be their first port of call. But then, ironically, like the Davisons, they chose to set up a more permanent base in Juan-les-Pins. As his biographer, Christopher Irmscher, wryly and pointedly, notes, it was *'a sun-warmed, lush Mediterranean paradise, a Sochi without communists'*.[10] It must be assumed that, at the time, Max was also aware that neighbouring Juan-les-Pins was emerging as a pulsating, offbeat resort and increasingly popular with American expatriates and sundry free spirits. It was just the sort of place for libidinous and bacchanalian revelries. And all the more so, since two of his acquaintances were living it up there – Scott Fitzgerald and Ernest Hemingway. It was time to party.

One problem for Max and his ever-accommodating wife was money. With funds rapidly running out, Eliena was obliged to secure a regular salary by taking up a clerical position in Paris. In the meantime, Max stayed on in Juan-les-Pins to write. Still insisting that his marriage remain an open one, he continued to indulge himself; this time, reputably, with a 'bushy-haired tennis partner'. He was presumably 'volleying' with her when he accepted an invitation from Davison to join Xmas celebrations at his, by now, fully reconstructed residence. Max clearly felt at home. His biographer described the occasion thus:

'... twenty-nine guests from ten nations had assembled at the house, and things quickly got out of hand. Max danced till five in the morning, no doubt working on his romance with "Bushy Hair", who had told him she was the daughter of a marquis, inspiring a fantasy in which Max acted the part of the seedy 'Bolshevik Agent' and she that of a besieged, virginal aristocrat'.

More prosaically, whether or not George Davison found the opportunity to discuss the likely impact of Stalin's rise to power seems highly unlikely. Max clearly had his mind on other things. Reflecting on Eastman's visit to the Davison's, his biographer does not hold back in a decidedly forthright passage. After dismissing Davison as 'an eccentric leftist photographer', he says of Eastman himself:

'The man who liked to refer to his lovers as children wholeheartedly embraced the notion of a house dedicated to the idea of permanently arrested development and had no problem partaking of Davison's hospitality. The Château des Enfants served as an open house for many sorts of washed-up artistic existences and anarchists from all over the world'.

In his text 'Rhythm and Colour', in which he describes the work of Margaret Morris, as well as the dancers who assisted her, the aforementioned Lois Hutton and Hélène Vanel, the writer Richard Emerson, notes that Max Eastman was also one of those visitors to the Grand Hôtel du Cap who greatly enjoyed watching the young girls attending the summer school. Ever true to lascivious form, Eastman is quoted as saying:

'Those girls were all excellent swimmers and each was in some delicately individual way moulded to fit ravishingly into a bathing suit'.

Villa Soleil, Grand Hôtel du Cap and Château des Enfants

Max and Eliena would stay on in Juan-les-Pins for a few more years, before finally moving back to Paris, and then in 1927 returning home to America.[11] As for Margaret Morris, she would repeat her Summer Schools at Cap d'Antibes for a couple more years, and in so doing would link up again with the Davisons and the management of the Grand Hôtel du Cap. But with the Great Depression looming, and prices in the locality rising rapidly, it was time for all concerned to call it a day. Also causing a re-think in 1929 was a fire that destroyed much of the pinewoods that surrounded Château des Enfants. According to Morris, George Davison never really recovered from the shock of it all. He died the following year and was buried in Antibes. As for his domain, it would eventually become part of the Grand Hôtel du Cap, with the villa changing its name to '*La Résidence*'. A brief but very lively episode in the annals of Cap d'Antibes had come to an abrupt end.[12]

In an interview with André Sella, the journalist M.C. Murphy, recalled him making the following observation concerning the social changes that had manifest themselves in the calibre of the hotel's clientele over time.

> "... *my father bought the hotel in 1888 it was for the express purpose of catering to the British and Russian aristocracy – the Russian grand dukes, that is. Well, you know what has happened to the Russian aristocracy. And every year the dukes and earls of England have grown a little poorer. In my own lifetime, I have seen the Spanish grandees, the German and Italian nobility wiped out. Along with them vanished the hereditary classes of the Austro-Hungarian Empire, as well as the old French aristocracy. Then in the great depression I saw the American millionaires brought down. As each class was subtracted the character of my hotel was affected.*
>
> *Moreover the hotel's function has in my lifetime been reversed. It started as a winter resort. The Edwardians, who regarded it as a breach of manners for a man to be seen in public with his coat off, had no choice but to leave the Côte d'Azur with the coming of the*

summer heat. So the hotel was closed all summer. Now we are open in the summer and closed in the winter.

No, nothing concerning the rich is fixed in this world. It would not surprise me at all to see the Riviera under the communists".[13]

The latter prognostication, clearly made in jest, may not have come about, but other Russians of very different political persuasions and backgrounds would choose to settle on Cap d'Antibes (see 5).

Villa Soleil, Grand Hôtel du Cap and Château des Enfants

It was Sophie's brother, Paul, who initiated the formative involvement of the Fersens in the development of Cap d'Antibes as a place of exclusive residence. Before settling in the area, Paul had been an *aide-de-camp* to Tsar Alexander II. Just two years later, aged 35 he also died. Paul had a son and daughter. Adding yet another layer of genealogical complexity, they were to be named Paul and Sophie. It was Villa Fersen that various members of the respective families would use as a base.

Enterprising, and with entrepreneurial drive, Paul von Fersen (junior) quickly sought out investment opportunities. Mindful of the steady growth in tourism elsewhere along the coast, and the positive impact that this was having on local property markets and economies, it was not long before he turned his gaze on Cap d'Antibes. At the time, as previously noted, the promontory was still a thinly populated and largely rural space, but one that was on the cusp of significant change in regard to prospective residential development. Lacking in rudimentary services and with a basic infrastructure, land was incredibly cheap and Ferson was in a position to buy up plots at rock-bottom prices. But in order to realise his grand plans, which envisaged the construction of substantial villas on sizeable plots, it was evident that venture capital would have to be sought from outside sources. This being the case, Fersen travelled to England and Holland hoping to seek out the necessary financial backing. In this he failed. However, Fersen would not have seen his schemes through to completion in any case. Within a few years, at the age of 36, he passed away, just two years after his sister Sophie. Not that his endeavours were entirely in vain. Before his untimely death, he had been instrumental in forwarding the construction of a new roadway leading into the heart of the promontory. It would later be improved and extended by others, and eventually become the *Boulevard du Cap*.[2] Fersen's early demise did not put an end to the wider family's involvement in private property development and the setting out of substantial *'domaines'*. Most significantly, and as previously recounted, Plestcheyev would soon join the consortium responsible for the establishment of what was to become the Grand Hôtel du Cap (see 3).

Unlike the Fersens and Plestcheyevs, the extended Russian family with which we are here particularly concerned (the Nikolaevichi branch of the Romanovs, together with Montenegrin relatives) was not in any way entrepreneurial; indeed, even if they had had the wherewithal, the pursuit of such matters would presumably have been deemed somewhat beneath their respective titles and associated statuses – even though the latter were by now essentially null and void. 'Former people' they may have been, but given what they and their homeland had just been through, and the enormity of their fall, the presence of noble Russian exiles added a short but highly distinctive chapter to the cultural history of Cap d'Antibes.

Dramatis Personae

The heads of the two households around whom the family history pivots were brothers, and grandsons of Tsar Nicholas I. The eldest was Grand Duke Nicholas Nikolaevich – statuesque, assured, influential, opinionated, deeply pious and, in certain circles, widely admired. Familiarly known as Nikolasha, he was a commanding presence: a military man through and through. For a short but inauspicious period at the beginning of World War I he was commander-in-chief of the Russian Imperial Army. The other was Grand Duke Peter Nikolaevich. More reserved than his outspoken brother, he too had pursued a career in the army, but his main interest in life, apart from his family, was a fascination with Middle Eastern architecture. Encouraged by his wife, for a time he also immersed himself in matters mystical – the occult. Frail of constitution, Peter suffered from pulmonary ailments, with a tubercular condition having long dogged him. In an effort to improve his health in his younger days he had paid a number of visits to the Middle East and the Maghreb. While there he would spend much of his stay sketching buildings and monuments of

Russians and Montenegrins in Exile

Grand Duke Nicholas

Princess Anastasia of Montenegro

Grand Duke Peter

Princess Milica of Montenegro

distinction. The trips sparked an interest that would remain with him throughout his life. It was partly because of his poor health that in the 1880s and 90s Peter had often made his way to the Côte d'Azur.[3]

The two brothers would not give the impression of having been cut from the same block, but they remained close throughout their lives. As if to underline the strength of their affinity they would both eventually end up with spouses who were sisters.

Whilst it might have been expected of them to marry into the higher echelons of the European Gotha, Nicholas and Peter actually married somewhat beneath their status – at least in the minds of those haughtily immersed in courtly Imperial society. Not that the marriages were morganatic or with first cousins – as had been problematically the case for certain other members of the wider Romanov family. It was just that the ladies involved – Militza Nikolaevna (Milica in Montenegrin) and Anastasia Nikolaevna by name – were princesses from a minor, far off place called Montenegro, set in the dark, misty heart of the Balkans.

After a troubled relationship with the Ottoman Empire, Montenegro had succeeded in asserting its independence, first as a Principality (1860-1910) and then as a Kingdom (1910-1918).[4] Guiding his country through these often very fractious times was the sisters' father Nicholas (Nikola) of the House of Petrovic. A committed Francophile, he had been busy gaining an education in Paris, at the acclaimed Lycée Louis-le-Grand, when in 1860, at the age of 19, he was unexpectedly pronounced the new ruler of Montenegro, following the assassination of his uncle Danilo I, to whom he was heir. Soon after returning home, Nikola married Milena Vukotic, the then illiterate daughter of a prominent landowner. They had been betrothed from a very early age, and at the time of their marriage Milena (as she was then known) was still only 14. From the outset, Nikola sought to further longstanding relations with Russia. Apart from the strong Slavic and Orthodox bonds, for Russia in particular there were geopolitical issues at

King Nicholas I of Montenegro   Queen Milena

play. Montenegro occupied a strategic position within the troubled Balkans, a region in which Russia had long held an interest. Not without good reason did Tsar Alexander III say of Prince Nicholas (as he was then styled) that *'he was the sole true and loyal friend of Russia'*.[5]

On a personal front, Nicholas and his wife began building an extensive family, embracing in the end a veritable brood of nine daughters and three sons. The second and third eldest of the princesses were Militza and Anastasia.[6] They were destined to become the respective spouses of Grand Duke Peter and Grand Duke Nicholas. The manner in which the said marriages came about were very different, but presumably would never have taken place at all had both young ladies not spent time receiving schooling and appropriate grooming in the prestigious Smolny Institute for Noble Maidens in St Petersburg. Established in 1808, it claimed to provide *'an ideal preparation for aspiring young brides'*. The Montenegrin princesses, together with another of their sisters – Elena (Helen) – had been invited to receive instruction at the said institute following earlier visits made by their father to Russia in 1868 and 1869. Over the coming years the sisters would slowly insert themselves into the *'beau monde'* of St Petersburg.

It has been suggested by some that their marriage was arranged, but, whatever the truth of the matter, in 1889 Militza and Grand Duke Peter exchanged vows. She was then 23 years of age. Their relationship proved to be close and long-lasting. They would remain together for some 42 years. In that time they had four children: Sophia who died at birth, Princess Marina, Prince Roman and Princess Nadejda. Interestingly, Marina was actually born in Nice whilst the family were sojourning on the Côte d'Azur for the winter season in 1891/92 (see below).

Anastasia (Stana) was initially much less fortunate in her choice of partner. He was George Maximilianovich Romanovsky,[7] the youngest of seven children born to Tsar Alexander II's sister, Maria Nikolaevna. George had previously been married to Duchess Therese Petrovna of Oldenburg, and as a consequence later became the 6th Duke of Leuchtenberg. His wife, of German stock, had grown up in Russia and, to all intents and purposes, was treated as a member of the Imperial family. Despite his waywardness the couple succeeded in having two sons, Alexander (7th Duke of Leuchtenberg) and Sergei (8th

Duchess Therese of Oldenburg

Duke of Leuchtenberg). Therese died in 1883, just four years into the marriage.[8] She was then 31 years of age.

It was six years after his wife's death that George married Anastasia. Once again it would prove to be a fraught coupling. George's unseemly behaviour certainly aroused the ire of Tsar Alexander III, and it was little surprise to all concerned when Anastasia decided to call it a day. The couple divorced in 1906. The following year Anastasia was more than delighted to secure the hand in marriage of Grand Duke Nicholas. The wedding ceremony took place not in St Petersburg, but away from it all in Yalta on the Crimean Peninsula. The two sisters and two brothers would thereafter form a tightly bonded family unit. Over the years to come they were to weather numerous storms together.

Within high society, it has to be said, the Montenegrin sisters were not widely liked. In the view of many, they were far too full of themselves, and tedious sticklers when it came to the issue of precedence in court circles. The Tsar's younger sister, Grand Duchess Olga Alexandrovna (1882 -1960) referred to them as '*Scylla and Charybdis, and nobody dared to make a move until the Montenegrin ladies were where they considered they should be*'. A particular bone of contention was the manner in which they ingratiated themselves with Tsar Nicholas's wife – Alexandra, fatefully encouraging her emerging interest in occultism. The latter, it was claimed, caused the highly-strung Tsarina to become too easily besotted with charlatans – for example, the French clairvoyant – Phillippe Nizier-Vashod, and worst of all, the *starets* Gregory Rasputin. In his memoir '*Lost Splendour*', Prince Felix Yousoupov [9] said of the sisters that they were surrounded by '*soothsayers and questionable prophets*', and that: '*Their palace was the central point of the powers of evil which so tragically bewitched our unhappy Tsar and Tsarina and plunged our country into the abyss*'. Yousoupov may have had an axe to grind, but an even more sympathetic source – a Serbian/Montenegrin foreign minister – recognised that '*a touch of malice*' was indeed a characteristic of the two sisters. The same source added, however, that assessments of their personalities were often *'over-simplified.'*[10]

It has been argued that the sisters' behaviour was mainly to gain favour and preference within the Imperial court; others were more concerned that it was for wider political reasons – their indirect aim being to influence appointments, policies and decision-making at the highest level. There was also talk that they were forever out to secure funds and favours for the Principality (Kingdom) of Montenegro. Little wonder then that the sisters were often referred to as the 'Black Crows' or the 'Black Peril'.[11] That they would later recognise the error of their ways, particularly in regard to Rasputin and his influence on the Tsarina (and thereby a compliant Tsar) cut no ice. It was all too late – by then the revolutionary die had already been cast, and fatefully so for all concerned.

But it was not just Anastasia and Militza who had ruffled Imperial feathers. Grand Duke Nicholas himself had annoyed many back in 1905 when in response to public unrest he had argued vehemently in support of reforms to the prevailing political order, and in so doing had forced the Tsar, with gun to hand, to accede to the establishment of a State Duma. However, Nicholas himself decided that, under the prevailing political circumstances, it would not be appropriate to accept an invitation from the Tsar to become commander–in-chief of the armed forces, the position from which he (the Tsar) had once so ignominiously dismissed him. Thenceforth, for Russia and the dynasty that had ruled for over six centuries, it was downhill all the way. With the political situation deteriorating as Bolshevism gained sway, and with the ensuing Civil War wreaking havoc across the land, it was hardly surprising that more and more people would seek to get as far away from the turmoil as possible. Many of those who feared for their lives, let alone livelihoods, headed south to the Crimean Peninsula. The Nikolaevichi clan joined them. Although they had other far more important concerns on their minds, Nicholas and his wife no doubt felt particularly aggrieved at having to take their leave of their recently completed palace back in St Petersburg, overlooking the Neva River and close to the St Peter and Paul Fortress. Likewise his brother Peter and Militza would have to say goodbye to the Znamensky Palace and its impressive gardens and grounds located outside the city, on the Peterhof Road. From now on, neither family would be receiving the great and the good sweeping elegantly through their stately porticos.

Journey into Exile

Unlike the many thousands of their compatriots who sought to escape the mayhem, as Red and White forces vied for control, the Nikolaevichi were fortunate to own second homes (palaces in reality) in the Koreiz district of the Crimea, some 9 miles to the south of Yalta. The domain, named Chaïr (meaning 'mountain garden' in the local Tatar language), had been acquired by Grand Duke Nicholas's father, but for whatever reason was formally registered in Anastasia's name. Construction of the main residence was completed in 1902. It was to here that Nicholas, his wife (and the two children from her first marriage, Sergei and Elena) initially repaired. In happier days the place had frequently been abuzz with Romanov gatherings on the terrace that looked out over the Black Sea. Visitors were also enthralled by the impeccable rose garden and the views of the Ai-Petri Mountains in the background.

Nearby, Grand Duke Peter had, over the years, worked with an esteemed local architect (Nikolai Krasnov), to create an extravagant but truly eye-catching palace named Dulber (Diulber) – in translation 'beautiful'. Given Peter's particular obsession, the residence was ornately Moorish in style, with cupolas, castellated parapets, colourful ornamentation and mosaics.

It was while they were holed up in Dulber Palace that Peter's daughter, Princess Nadejda, was married in April 1917, and in the very place where she had been born some 20 years earlier.[12] Interestingly, her husband-to-be was Nikolai Orlov, the son of the prominent military advisor to Tsar Nicholas II – Vladimir Orlov.

Chaïr Palace

Dulber Palace

However, vehemently and outspokenly opposed to Rasputin as a malign influence, he too eventually fell out of imperial favour, and was summarily dismissed from office. Vladimir also happened to be a particularly close friend of Grand Duke Nicholas, and was presumably quite happy to join up with him, when he (Nicholas) was appointed governor-general of the Caucasus. They must have made an odd-looking pairing – Nicholas, lean and exceedingly tall, whilst Vladimir was short and vastly overweight. One writer described Orlov as – *'the obese giant'* (sic) who *'resembled the Porthos of Dumas's novel'*.[13] However, both were energetic and committed to the Imperial cause.[14]

Scattered around the southern shores of the Crimea at this time were other prominent members of the wider Romanov family, together with a medley of aristocrats and nobles, all waiting to see how the Civil War – the ever-fluctuating fortunes of the Red and White armies, and the jockeying for position of local soviets, would play themselves out. The clash between the Sebastopol and Yalta soviets was particularly disturbing, for the fate of the Romanovs depended on which of them would gain the upper hand. It would be an unnerving situation, and in the end a very close call for all involved. By the spring of 1918, with the situation rapidly deteriorating by the day, it was evident that exile was now the only option.[15] Concerned about the future, and with Grand Duke Nicholas no longer being in receipt of his annual stipend from the Tsar, in May that year Anastasia decided to sell Chaïr. Under the circumstances, she was fortunate to find a buyer – a wealthy factory owner from the Urals, named Ivanov, who was also a Member of the Council of Ministers.[16] When it came to accepting the inevitable, the Dowager Empress, Maria Feodorovna (widow of Tsar Alexander III), who had been living nearby with members of her own family, initially demurred, but in the end reluctantly accepted the parlousness of the collective situation. The final moves of the endgame were about to be played. By now, with everyone corralled in the Dulber Palace for their own safety, and with danger lurking all around, those concerned hurriedly readied themselves to board the British battleship HMS Marlborough that had been sent to secure their escape from what was now a war zone. They did not know it at the time, but they would never return to live out their remaining years in Mother Russia. It was a mournful farewell for all concerned.

After crossing the Black Sea, and threading its way through the Bosphorus Straits, HMS Marlborough halted at Halki Island, off Constantinople. The voyage was largely uneventful, but longstanding tensions between the Dowager Empress and Grand Duke Nicholas still bubbled quietly below the public surface. However, on the part of both parties, efforts were made to behave *'comme il faut'* – it was a family matter, *'noblesse oblige'*. That said, it was tacitly acknowledged that for the onward journey the Nikolaevichi should chart their own course into exile. But, for them, there was still some confusion as to where they might finally end up. It had been made clear, in no uncertain terms, that, unlike the Dowager Empress and those close to her, they would not be welcome in Britain. Resolution of the impasse subsequently came in the form of an invitation from the Italian government for them to settle in Italy. Of key significance in securing this invitation was undoubtedly the fact that Queen Elena of Italy was sister to Anastasia and Militza. It will be recalled that she had also spent time with them in the Smolny Institute in St Petersburg, so knew full well how 'noble maidens' should behave! Like her father, Nikola, Elena proved to be more than competent as a linguist, loved poetry and displayed considerable political awareness. In 1896, at the age of 23 she had married Victor Emmanuel, then Prince of Naples.[17] Four years later he would be crowned King of Italy. Elena was universally held in high regard for her commitment to the nation, and for her unstinting work in aid of the poor and the needy.[18] In her interests and abilities she may have differed greatly from her sisters, but she most certainly would not let them down in a time of crisis. Indeed in the not too distant future she would find herself facing a similar dilemma (see below).

With agreement reached as to their final destination, the Nikolaevichi party, some 12 in number, transferred to another British battleship HMS Lord Nelson.[19] They would soon be on their way to the Italian port of Genoa. By all accounts, alone together for the first time, the families openly displayed their despondency at having to leave their homeland, and in such an unedifying fashion. Still struggling to come to terms with their predicament and the uncertainties that lay ahead, the group eventually set foot on dry land in April 1919. Waiting to greet them and eager to catch up on all that had happened were King Victor Emmanuel and his consort. It must have been a highly emotional family reunion for all concerned. For not only had the Romanov branch been obliged to leave their homeland, so too had the sisters' father, King Nikola and members of his immediate family (see below). It was chaos all around. What to do and where to go? France was the preferred country, but an issue that would surface early on was where precisely to set up homes for the family at large, for there was no intention that they should now go their separate ways. They were too close for that, and had been through so much together.

One complicating factor was the pressure that Grand Duke Nicholas was under from various quarters to head up opposition to the Bolshevik government that was slowly, but fitfully, tightening its grip on power. An acknowledged leader was needed to ensure that material, moral and political support for the White Movement back home was effectively mobilised. The former commander-in-chief of the Russian Army was seen as just such a leader. Grand Duke Nicholas was an obvious choice. With more and more exiles electing to base themselves in Paris, the city inevitably became the focal point from which to launch a propaganda offensive from afar. But rather than settling in Paris itself, Nicholas chose to rent a small château some 20 kilometres outside of the city – Château Choigny. Although the residence also served as a home of sorts, it was essentially a centre of operations, and one appropriately guarded by a troop of Cossacks. With the French secret service also deployed to ensure his safety, and with a military pension to help ease financial woes, Nicholas began the task of serving the needs of the Russian community in exile. It would prove to be an exacting and, in the end, futile cause. The decision by the French government, then under the premiership of Édouard Herriot, to establish diplomatic relations with the USSR in 1924 was a truly devastating blow; one that would never be forgiven. Downhearted, Nicholas continued to struggle on, but no doubt as time went by he would look forward to spending more and more time in the South of France where, at the beginning of his period in exile, he had established a family home for himself, his brother and his kin, well away from the onerous pressures of life in Paris. Cap d'Antibes was ready to receive them. It certainly had much to offer, a restorative retreat, well away from it all.

Montenegrins and Nikolaevichi in Residence

Whilst Paris continued to serve a particular political purpose and was their formal base, both Nicholas and Peter appreciated that their wives would also wish to have family homes near their ageing parents who were also now living in exile. Their father, Nikola, former King of Montenegro, had sided with the Allies against the Central Powers in 1914, but with his kingdom quickly overrun by Austrian forces he had been obliged to seek sanctuary elsewhere. Unsurprisingly, as a committed Francophile, there was little doubt as to where he would elect to settle. Initially based in Bordeaux, where he set up a government-in-exile, and then moving on to Paris, the King and his wife, Milena, eventually decided, with their declining health in mind, to move to the shores of the Mediterranean. They too looked forward to returning home to Montenegro sometime, and hopefully in the not too distant future. Ex-king Nikola was confident that they would do so, for he had been assured that following an allied victory in the First World

War his royal authority would eventually be restored. However, geopolitical machinations were such that, despite earlier promises to the contrary, higher powers decided that Montenegro should lose its separate identity, and that its lands should be subsumed within a newly created territory, to be styled the Kingdom of Serbs, Croats and Slovenes (later Yugoslavia). Affronted but unbowed, King Nikola fought on, hoping to salvage what he could of the situation. It would be a vain hope – he would not be returning home to his 'Black Mountain' kingdom – at least not while he or his wife were alive.

Having heard of the particular attractions of Cap d'Antibes from their son and heir, Crown Prince Danilo, who had retreated to the locality earlier, together with his wife – Duchess Jutta of Mecklenburg-Strelitz,[20] it was here that the former King and Queen of Montenegro chose, in virtual retirement, to establish a new home and campaign base. By this time, however, his finances were sorely depleted, and the villa that he eventually acquired – 'Les Liserons' – was a very modest affair. Locals were apparently surprised that a member of royalty should only be able to afford such a meagre property – a circumstance made all the more glaring by the substantial mansions by then featuring on Cap d'Antibes. Not only that, the ex-king was reputed not even to have a car at his disposal.[21] If this caused him any embarrassment, then it would not be for long; for in March 1921 he died of a cerebral haemorrhage at the age of 80. To demonstrate, in part, their dismay and anger at France's lack of support for the restoration of their kingdom after the end of the Great War, the family pointedly decided to conduct the funeral service and burial in Italy. Ex-King Nikola's coffin was ceremoniously escorted to the nearby harbour at Antibes, from where it was taken aboard an Italian warship – the 'Palestro'. The burial service took place in the Orthodox Church at St Remo.

King Nikola's wife, Milena, stayed on at the villa after her husband's death. Also ailing, she was looked after by two of her other daughters, Vera and Xenia. She died just two years after her husband, and was buried with him at St Remo.[22] Vera was still living at the family villa when, despite the best efforts of a specialist Russian surgeon, she too died. She was 40 years of age, the year 1927. As for Danilo, who became the nominal King of Montenegro on his father's death, he had then, contentiously and inexplicably, renounced his title. As it happened, he had earlier moved away from the rest of the family, having acquired a substantial domain further along the coast on Cap Martin – Le Mas d'Aréthuse. Later he would relocate, to a property he had purchased in the settlement of Roquebrune, just a short distance from Cap Martin. Danilo was not to end his days on the Côte d'Azur, however, for he died in 1939 while in Vienna, a year after the Austrian Anschluss.

When he first took up residence on Cap d'Antibes, Grand Duke Nicholas rented Villa Taormina, a property owned by a former mayor of Antibes – Gustave Chancel (in office 1901-1914). It will be recalled that this residence would later come into the ownership of Aga Khan III (see 1). However, the family's stay there was to be short, for they then moved into a much more substantial residence – an imposing four-storey residence set in four hectares of gardens, and located in the heart of the Cap d'Antibes – Château Thénard.[23] Conveniently, it fronted, but was set back from, the Boulevard du Cap that linked Antibes with the Hôtel du Cap-Eden-Roc. Not that they or the '*clientele fortunée*' who were descending on the area in increasing numbers were likely to make use of it, since from 1902 onwards an electric tramway established by '*La Compagnie des Transports de Nice et du Littoral*' had operated through the heart of the cape, as far as the Grand Hôtel du Cap. In 1930 this service was terminated, and replaced by a bus schedule.

For Nicholas and Anastasia the location would have been particularly appealing, for all around there were commercial flower-growing smallholdings, including many specialising in roses. Such was the importance of floriculture in the wider region that during the 1890s the locality was frequently referred to in promotional literature as '*Antibes-les-Fleurs*'. No doubt the colour and the

Château Thénard

fragrance would have reminded the couple of the rose garden that that they had created and so cherished at Chaïr in the Crimea, and which they had been obliged to sell.[24] It has been suggested that Château Thénard was actually paid for by Queen Elena of Italy, Anastasia's aforementioned sister, but others have claimed that the family first rented the property and had later decided to purchase it themselves.[25] However, whilst the Grand Duke continued to busy himself with promoting anti-Bolshevik causes, Anastasia became heavily involved in numerous charitable projects. She was a patron of the Overseas Union of Russian Military Invalids, and took a particular interest in events organised in aid of those Russians, members of Wrangel's defeated White Army forces, who were now facing difficulties in exile. After their evacuation from the Crimea many found themselves confined to camps on the Gallipoli peninsula. Anastasia also lent her support to the convalescent home for exiled Russians in Menton – the Brotherhood of St Anastasia.

As for Grand Duke Peter, he took up residence in Villa Donatello, close to his brother's property. It was sizeable but not as grand. Here he spent much of his leisure time painting – especially scenes of a religious and historical nature. Presumably, his days dabbling in the occult were long gone. For whatever reason, it was at Château Thénard in 1921 that the marriage service and wedding reception of Peter's son, Roman, to Countess Prascovia Demitrieva Sheremeteva was held. She was aged 20, Roman 25. The venue

Prince Roman and Countess Prascovia

may still have been quite impressive, but it was a far cry from where it might have been held, and the invitees who would have been in attendance, had the couple been back in Russia, for Countess Prascovia was a scion of one of the most noble and wealthy of families in Russia. Her father, Count Dimitri Scheremetev, had been aide-de-camp to Tsar Nicholas II, whilst her mother, Irina, was of equally notable Vorontsov-Dashkov lineage.

The Scheremetevs themselves had escaped from Russia at the same time as the Nikolaevichi. They first sequestered in the Caucasus, had succeeded in making a dramatic escape from there, and had somehow made their way to the Crimea where most of them stayed at the imposing Vorontsov-Dashkov palace. They left Yalta on the same day as the imperial family (11th April, 1919), but with the boys and girls of the family being separated. Together with their father, Dimitri, the three boys boarded the British destroyer 'Speedy', whilst the girls – also three in number – joined their mother, Irina, on another vessel, the 'Inna'. The two groups came together again on the Princes' Islands in the Sea of Marmara, opposite Constantinople. After meeting up with, and commiserating with, the Dowager Empress's party and other Russians crowding into the area at that time, they moved on and eventually sought exile in France. Thus it was that they ended up on the Côte d'Azur. Here they would recuperate for a while, catching their breath after a truly harrowing adventure. Fortunately, the family had

Marina Golitsyn   Alexander Golitsyn

managed to bring some shares in a Baku-based oil company and with this asset were in a position to purchase a modest property. As it happened, Prascovia's mother, Irina, still owned a villa not far from the Nikolaevichi's residence on Cap d'Antibes.[26] It was there that Prascovia and Roman were to plight their troth. The couple were still in Antibes when in 1926 they had their first child – Dimitri Romanovich.[27] The family would later move on and settle with Prascovia's parents in Rome.

Six years after Roman's marriage, it was his sister Marina Petrovna Golitsyna who would wed. Her fiancé was Prince Alexander Nikolaevich Golitsyn, the son of Nicolai Dmitrievich Golitsyn. Unfortunately, his father would not be present at the ceremony. Some two years earlier, back in St Petersburg, he had been executed. For a brief period of time, he had held the dubious honour of having been Imperial Russia's last prime minister. Accused of counter-revolutionary activity, he was put to death in 1925.[28] It must be assumed that at least Prince Alexander's mother – née Evgenia Andrejevna von Grünberg – would have been able to attend the ceremony since she was resident in the area. It was in Nice that she died in July 1934. The newly-weds were to remain living on the Côte d'Azur, eventually setting up home near Toulon in a villa that had been purchased for them by Evgenia's generous aunt, Queen Elena of Italy. While there, Princess Marina, who was a trained and accomplished painter, continued with her work. But the couple's finances were clearly somewhat stretched. More recently, Philippe Koutseff – president of '*Amitiés russes de Provence*' – reminisced that his father, who had been a doctor in the Toulon area, had also managed to escape Russia. He was greatly impressed with Marina. Of her, he said: '*Elle vivait secrètement, portant en elle la noblesse de ses ancêtres, élevant des poules et des chèvres dans sa villa*'. ['She lived secretly, displaying the nobility of her ancestors, while looking after chickens and goats at her villa']. Marina died in 1981 and was pre-deceased by her husband, Alexander in 1974. Following tradition they were both buried in the Russian cemetery at Caucade in Nice.[29]

It will be recalled that the first of Peter's children to marry was Nadejda, and that before having to leave Russia with the rest of her family, she had given birth to Irina in 1918. Four years later, while living in exile, the couple had another daughter Xenia. The marriage eventually foundered, and in 1940 they were divorced.

In terms of links with Cap d'Antibes one final association is worthy of brief reference. It concerns the acclaimed writer Vladimir Nabokov.[30] With political disturbances mounting in St Petersburg his family decided to escape the turmoil by moving south to the Crimea. They stayed there until early 1919, all the while hoping that conditions would improve. They did not. Indeed they became ever more precarious. Reluctantly, like so many others, they were obliged to leave their homeland and to join them in exile. In their case the move was first to London, and then onto Berlin where his father had been accidently killed in a politically motivated assassination attempt on a fellow Russian. Vladimir eventually ended up on the Côte d'Azur near Menton. In a state of penury, and still attempting to make a living for himself as a writer, in August 1938 he moved along the coast to Cap d'Antibes, having heard of a pension offering accommodation to destitute Russian exiles. Of interest here, in a biography, the author Brian Boyd notes that the residence concerned, Villa les Cyprès by name, was *'a grand house in the middle of the slender peninsula'*, adding that it had previously been a private residence – *'the property of the Duke of Leichtenberg (a Russian despite his name)'*. He then adds that *'it was now the "Russian, very Russian" – House of the Union of the St George Cross for Disabled Veterans'*.[31] It is clear that there is a misspelling here, for 'Leichtenberg' should surely be 'Leuchtenberg'. No indication is given as to whether or not it was the 7th or 8th Duke to whom it once belonged as a family home. It could have been either Anastasia's stepson – the aforementioned Alexander Georgevich or her son – Sergei Georgevich – 8th Duke of Leuchtenberg.[32] Both were with her at Cap d'Antibes at around that time.

Appropriately enough, Villa les Cyprès was located on a narrow winding road named *'Chemin de l' Ermitage'*. Vladimir would not stay for long. He soon moved along the coast and for a time settled with his wife and child in Cannes.

The End of an Era

In November 1928 Grand Duke Nicholas left his chateau in Paris for good and headed south to his home on Cap d'Antibes. He was suffering from a chest infection and hoped that spending the winter months in a more soothing environment would ease his condition. Unfortunately, the weather did not help matters, for unseasonable snowstorms swept across the locality. Nicholas caught pneumonia, and although he was able to celebrate Xmas with some dignity, he failed to recover. In the first week of January, aged 72, he died. At his bedside, together with members of his close family, were Prince Andrew of Russia – the son of Tsar Nicholas's sister Xenia and her husband, Grand Duke Alexandrovich Mikhailovich (Sandro). He too had left Russia with his father via the Crimea, and for some time had settled in exile on the Riviera. After a requiem held in 'Saint Michael the Archangel' in Cannes, the old warhorse was laid to rest in its chapel. Many prominent members of the dwindling Russian community in exile attended his funeral. Appropriately, Cossacks formed an imposing guard of honour for the grandest of grand dukes. They would have been proud of the fact that at his passing he chose to be garbed in the uniform of the Caucasian Cossacks. Among the various foreign dignitaries at the burial service was his friend Maréchal Pétain – the Lion of Verdun, and then head of the French Army in peacetime.

Also present at the service was the acclaimed Russian writer Ivan Bunin. Living in exile nearby, in the hill town of Grasse, he

Grand Duke Nicholas – Cortège (Villa Thénard)

Ivan Bunin

was a particularly vehement critic of Bolshevism. He had left Russia at the very last moment, boarding a boat from Odessa where, ever true to his beliefs, he had been working for the Voluntary Army. A monarchist and staunch supporter of the old Imperial order, he left Russia in disgust and dismay at how the country had been torn apart by leftist factions. Not mincing his words, he would later describe Lenin as *'a bastard and an idiot'*. Bunin's wife would later recall how deeply upset he was at the passing of Grand Duke Nicholas. The knell, he proclaimed, was finally tolling for Mother Russia.

Bunin's mood must have been lifted some four years later, however, for he was the first Russian writer to be awarded the Nobel Prize for literature for his novellas, tales and critical writings. Disarmingly pellucid and poised in style, and with a rhythm of their own, they probed the human condition and said much about social and economic issues in his homeland. The literary award was a singular achievement for someone who counted Tolstoy, Chekhov and, for a while at least, Maxim Gorky, amongst his acquaintances. As it happened, the writers Tolstoy, Gogol, Turgenev and Chekov had all previously been visitors to the Côte d'Azur, but in their cases for very different reasons. Interestingly, Bunin would later make a number of trips to Cap d'Antibes. On these occasions, however, he would be spending time at the Russian House in Juan-les-Pins – a clinic for those, like himself, suffering from various ailments and in need of convalescence. However, it was in Paris, in 1953, that he would take his last breath – aged 83 years.

Grand Duke Peter was the central mourner at his brother's funeral. Together, they had lived through a most convulsive period in Russia's history; a period that bore witness to the evisceration of the Romanov family that had ruled over Russia for more than three centuries. But time was slowly taking its toll on the old guard. Just two years after the demise of his brother, Peter too would pass away. Appropriately, he would join him in the crypt in Cannes.

Anastasia continued to soldier on at Château Thénard following the death of her husband, and it was here that she too died in 1935, aged 67. However, matters were not that straightforward as far as her sister Militza was concerned. In fact she was about to write another chapter in her tumultuous life. Following Peter's death, she elected to join her sister Elena in Rome. As previously observed, her son Roman and his family would join her there. But that would not be the end to her travels, or travails. The collapse of the Italian monarchy in 1946 meant that Militza, together with members of her immediate family, would again be seeking exile, this time in Egypt. It was here in 1951, in Alexandria, that she died at the age of 85. Her body was returned to France and finally laid to rest alongside that of her husband in Cannes. Finally, the two sets of brothers and sisters, who had led such close lives together, were reunited.

But the Nikolaevichi saga had not reached its dénouement. In 2015, following requests from Prince Roman's children – Nicholas Romanovich (Prince of Russia) and Prince Dimitri Romanovich of Russia – the remains of the grand dukes and duchesses, as well as those of their grandparents, were respectfully removed from the crypt in Cannes, where they were first laid to rest, and reburied in the Bratsky Military Cemetery in Moscow. It would be interesting to know what the opinionated Grand Duke Nicholas would have thought of the transfer. Mixed feelings no doubt. He was back home, but it was a very different place from that which so many of his kith and kin had been obliged, so hurriedly and so regretfully, to take their leave. Not to mention, of course, all those other Romanovs who, nearly a hundred years earlier, had failed to escape and had met a brutal end. Most notably they included Tsar Nicholas II and his family at the Ipatiev House in Yekaterinburg in July 1918.

To complete the picture, as far as Anastasia's sister, Elena, was concerned, she eventually left Egypt and returned to the south of France. Not to the Côte d'Azur, however, but not too far away. In need of medical attention she underwent treatment at the famed medical facilities in Montpellier. It was here in 1952, that she died, just a year after her sister. The former Queen of Italy was buried without great ceremony in the town's St Lazare municipal cemetery.[33] It marked the conclusion of what was a frantic and tragic family drama; one in which Cap d'Antibes was fortuitously to play a small, but not insignificant, part.

5
Oligarchs: Rise and Retreat

FOR THE RESORTS of the Côte d'Azur the ending of the Second World War saw a repeat of the readjustments made following that of the Great War (*La Grande Guerre*). A period of slow rehabilitation ensued, as economies sought to establish a new equilibrium. One manifestation of the steady recovery was a building boom that would transform landscapes and lives across the littoral. With land values rapidly rising, many landowners saw fit to cash in. Land had become a prized asset. One particular consequence was a widespread proliferation of high-rise developments. In the opinion of many, this had resulted in a tawdry despoliation of the landscape.[1] The wider Antibes region did not escape these changes, but their impress was less manifest, especially on its exclusive cape. However, slowly but surely, astute buyers of quality real estate returned. Perhaps not surprisingly, the majority were from foreign parts. However, noticeable by their absence were Russians.

With the Soviet Union's borders more firmly closed than ever before, and with a Cold War unnerving the situation, it was hardly surprising that their presence was far from being what it once was. Restrictions on foreign travel, currency issues and economic constraints meant that, as in former years, most would now be making their regimented way down to state-controlled spas and sanatoria along the shores of the Crimean Peninsula and in select parts of the Caucasus. Ironically, and as previously described, the vast majority of the great palaces, villas and *'domaines'*, once owned by those who sought exile in the early 1920s, had been summarily nationalised. Of these, a goodly number were turned into hospitals and places of convalescence. Dulber, Grand Duke Peter's magnificent retreat, for example, became the first Soviet sanatorium. Later, Chaïr, the former residence of his brother, Grand Duke Nicholas, experienced a similar fate and was converted into an orphanage.

Over the decades that followed, containment and closure prevailed until yet another quasi-revolutionary event transformed everything, virtually overnight. It was an event that would have major ramifications on the international political front but, bizarrely, as it was to turn out, it was also one that would have remarkable, if indirect, repercussions for the whole of the Côte d'Azur, and for Cap d'Antibes in particular. Up until the coming to power of President Mikhail Gorbachev in 1985, the Union of Soviet Socialist Republics (Soviet Union) seemed solid and immutable. Following his accession, however, efforts were made to reform deep-rooted ideological systems (perestroika and glasnost). But it proved to be a change too far and too fast. A period of chaos and uncertainty ensued. Hoping that he would be able to steady and to reorient the ship, Boris Yeltsin was elected president of the Russian Federation in 1991 and remained in post until 1999. With less onerous restrictions on foreign travel in place, resorts throughout the Côte d'Azur looked forward to welcoming more and more visitors from Russia and the satellite states. With luck hotel registers in particular would record increasing numbers of Slavic names. Concomitantly, it was expected that there would be an upsurge in demand for real estate. This would prove to be the case, but perhaps more slowly, and more limited in focus than first expected.

Oddly, it was another series of developments during this period of political uncertainty that was to have a high profile impact on the Russian presence in the region. The resignation of President Gorbachev, the incumbency of Boris Yeltsin, and the chaotic privatisation (expropriation) of once state-owned assets (industries, natural resources, the media and sundry services) that ensued, opened the door to the emergence of a new oligarchy of entrepreneurs, many of whom would see opportunities for investing some of their vast, new-found wealth, on the Côte d'Azur. Virtually *ab initio*, a Russian plutocracy had been forged; one that in its purchasing power more than rivalled that of the Romanovs and the industrial, mining and railway barons of the *'ancien régime'*. The august titles of times past may have been missing, but to all intents and purposes they were an emergent nobility; latter-day grand dukes in all but name. Although relatively limited in number, such was their wealth and general extravagance that it could only serve to re-affirm the abiding image of the Riviera as *'a sunny place for shady people'*, as the writer Somerset Maugham would once have it, while comfortably settled in his own sumptuous villa on Cap Ferrat.

As far as the resorts of the Côte d'Azur were concerned, the power of the oligarchs, and indeed of the lesser plutocrats who had benefitted from Yeltsin's unconscionable largesse, was from the very outset most starkly manifest in the changing dynamics of the very high-end property markets across the whole region. For those Russians of vast, newfound means, here was a haven where they could diversify, and hopefully shelter, their ever-expanding portfolio of assets. For those with a discerning eye, rich pickings were to be had in prime real estate. Not only that, what better way to flaunt one's newfound wealth than to acquire prestigious villas and associated *'domaines'* in places high in social cachet, and ideally hidden from the public gaze? Cap d'Antibes, and in particular its wooded southern tip, would soon enter the frame.

If the properties concerned were slightly down at heel and had perhaps been a little neglected by previous owners, no matter. Vast sums could be called upon to re-structure and refurbish as seen appropriate. Architects and designers of international renown could be readily enlisted to pamper to the flights of fancy of inordinately wealthy paymasters. If a particular property had ties, however tenuous, with Russia's past then so much the better. Perhaps a tsar or tsarina had at one time even crossed its portals, and taken genteel walks in what would soon be heavily guarded grounds. Whether or not such matters actually figured in oligarchic thinking is doubtful, but there were surely some who saw themselves as, in a sense, picking up batons that, back in Mother Russia, were so abruptly dropped by some of their renowned forebears – a gaining of further prestige through historical and nationalistic association. The 'ideological' and moral irony embedded in such thinking needs little elaboration. In especially favoured locations, such as Cap d'Antibes, they would soon be ruling the roost. Flitting around them would come sundry others; like bees around an increasingly Russianized honeypot.

An equally important consideration for those Russians investing so heavily in the area was the fact that the Côte d'Azur had somehow managed, despite intense international competition, to hold on to its longstanding reputation as a uniquely glamorous playground, even though the built environment at large was not as pristine as it once was. Over the years, a galaxy of starred restaurants, hotels, private clubs and casinos, not to mention a host of internationally acclaimed festivals, congresses and sporting events, had undoubtedly added to its allure.

Unsurprisingly, for many of the coastal resorts of the region, serving the multifarious needs of the global sailing fraternity was particularly high on the agenda. Harbours and marinas had to be upgraded and extended. At the same time, a medley of associated factors and services (e.g. training and provision of crews, leasing and insurance agents, specialised repairs and maintenance, quality victualing outlets) needed not only to be readily accessible, but also to meet the highest of standards.

Over recent decades, one particularly distinctive feature of the marine landscape throughout the Côte d'Azur, and one that would be associated in particular with Russian oligarchs, has been the high profile presence of so-called 'superyachts'; those that exceed 100 metres in length. Some would go so far as to refer to them as mega-yachts, or even 'giga-yachts'. Whatever their designations, many of these huge vessels are or have been, in the ownership of high-profile oligarchs. More recent political events, however, have seriously upset the *status quo* (see below). All that needs to be said at this particular juncture is that the superyachts concerned have had such huge sums lavished on their outward design and their interiors that they are to all intents and purposes 'floating palaces'. Not only that; such has been the inordinately high level of investment in associated security systems that they are also 'floating fortresses'. Collectively, these sea-going leviathans, and other vessels of marginally lesser status, would more than compete in elegance and sophistication with those in the ownership of wealthy Americans and Arabian royalty, both in the past and in more recent times. Of these vessels many have occupied feted berths in the port of Antibes, or at the very least have fleetingly been seen skirting Cap d'Antibes. Had Guy de Maupassant encountered them as he nursed his 11 foot cutter '*Bel Ami*' around the cape in the late 1880s he would no doubt have been astounded. But, given his attitude to affluence and the flaunting of wealth, it is unlikely that he would have been taken in by it all.

In view of the references made in the media to the oligarchs as 'latter-day grand dukes', it is worth noting that in the 1890s many members of the Romanov family, owned or leased sea-going vessels of significant size. TsarNicholas II himself was the proud owner of the 'Standart' (128 metres) and the 'Zarnitza' (118 metres), both of which would today be classed as superyachts. As can be imagined, in both these cases, interiors were exquisitely fitted and suitably ornamented, with highly polished mahogany throughout. Such was the high regard in which the 'Standart' was held, that a finely executed Fabergé egg, one of 50 or so made over the years for Tsar Alexander III and Tsar Nicholas II, was specifically dedicated to it. As an aside, the esteemed egg is thought to have escaped being sold on the open market and is still in Russian hands. At the time, both yachts were often to be seen cruising the shores of the Côte d'Azur. More often than not, those on board would be regally feted when in harbour.

The issue of the superyachts will surface later in a more contentious context, but at this point attention turns to the history and ownership of a number of prime properties on Cap d'Antibes, which came into the ownership of several prominent oligarchs.

A Russian Enclave

Whilst Grand Dukes Nicholas and Peter were very conscious of their heritage and the need to maintain standards of etiquette that respected their titles, as exiles they were not in a position to live the materially privileged life that they once had. As for their personal security, a few faithful Cossacks would now have to suffice. But, while resident on Cap d'Antibes, this did not mean that they found it necessary to cut themselves off totally from the local community. To a degree, they sought to engage. The same cannot be said of those Russians who, sixty years or so later, would buy up and extravagantly renovate highly prized '*domaines*' on the cape. As previously noted, to them seclusion and personal security were of paramount importance. However, this did not mean that jet-setting oligarchs were not averse to openly courting and entertaining celebrities of international standing. It was simply yet another opportunity to flaunt their vast wealth and, at the same time, to cultivate contacts and to explore further investment opportunities.

But cracks would soon begin to appear in the whole oligarchic edifice. Over more recent times, awkward questions have increasingly been asked concerning such matters as tax avoidance, sources of finance, possible money laundering, together with the use of off-shore accounts and shell companies. Inevitably, the acquisition and ownership of high-end real estate and superyachts would enter the frame of scrutiny. But, out of the blue, there would be much more to contend with.

(i) Boris Berezovsky and Château de la Garoupe

It will be recalled that in 1921 Cole Porter and his wife had rented Château de la Garoupe, located on the very tip of Cap d'Antibes. Celebrating their honeymoon, they had arrived in the area in midsummer and had chosen to stay for a short while.

Château de la Garoupe was built for Laura and Charles McLaren on land they had purchased in 1906. Their considerable fortune was derived initially from assets accumulated by Laura's father, Henry Davis Pochin. Until his death in 1895 he had steadily built a substantial business empire based on china clay mining, shipbuilding and iron and steel production. At the time, the site that they bought was untamed and covered in pine woodland. For the design of the residence the couple engaged the London-based architects, Sir Ernest George and Alfred Yates. Around the Italianate villa, the McLarens, both of whom were keen, knowledgeable and imaginative gardeners, began the process of clearing sections of the estate ready for landscaping and planting. Following the death of her parents, their daughter, Priscilla, inherited the property. She, together with her husband Sir Henry Norman, continued to work on the development of the grounds. Little wonder then that experts would soon come to regard the landscaping, design and planting regime as being of *'unfailing grandeur'* and *'astonishing beauty'*. As previously noted, an axial stairway running down to the rocky foreshore was a stunning and binding feature, as were the parterres, terraces and rich array of trees, succulents, shrubs and aromatic plantings. Not without reason, the entrance to the property once carried a carved inscription *'Lasciate ogni dolore – voi ch'entrate'* from Dante's Divine Comedy: Inferno, Canto 3. 'Let go of all pain – you who enter here'. No doubt, at the time, many did.

Château de la Garoupe remained in the ownership of the family up until 1996 when the property was sold to one of the most high profile of early Russian oligarchs – Boris Berezovsky – reputedly for just over 8 million euros. The following year, the separate but

Château de la Garoupe

attached property – Le Clocher de la Garoupe – became part of the estate, having been acquired for, according to some reports, a further 13.5 million euros.[2] As if this were not enough, yet another neighbouring villa and tract of land came into the oligarch's ownership for yet another enormous sum. The first two of these purchases were made at a time when Berezovsky held a position of considerable political prominence and power back home in Russia. In this, it certainly helped that Boris Yeltsin was a close friend and ally. So much so, that Yeltsin, together with members of his family, are known to have sojourned at Château de la Garoupe on numerous occasions.

With the coming to power of Vladimir Putin in 2000, however, the situation was soon to change. For a while, Berezovsky and Putin seemed to 'get on', but for a whole range of reasons, including the ownership of particular privatized assets and involvement in political matters beyond the remit demanded, the relationship foundered. The horrendous loss of the Kursk submarine in August 2000, with 118 personnel losing their lives, and the dilatory manner of the president's response to the crisis, was just one of many fractious, interpersonal arguments that rankled. Berezovsky berated the president for remaining *'en vacances'*, happily waterskiing at the Caucasian resort of Sochi, while the tragic and much publicized drama of the Kursk was unfolding. According to the journalist, Steven Lee Myers, Berezovsky at one point had phoned Putin from Château de la Garoupe, reputedly saying:

'Volodya, why are you in Sochi? You should interrupt your holiday and go to the submarine base, or at least to Moscow'.

Not to do so, he maintained, would seriously damage his presidency, which was then just a year old. Putin's response was apparently blunt. He had replied: *'And why are you in France?'*. Apparently, Berezovsky's response was to stress that he was not the nation's leader; adding, rather indelicately, that *'No one gives a **** where I am'*. But with this very particular clash and other much sharper differences of political opinion to follow, Berezovsky's fate was inevitably sealed. It was hardly surprising then, that he quickly fell from favour. More than that, in other quarters awkward questions were soon being asked about his wheeling and dealing, and his political machinations and private ambitions. Berezovsky came to realise that his time was up, and that he had to ready himself for beating a hasty retreat. In so doing, and with much irony, he would now be following in the footsteps of so many of his Romanov forebears, as well as thousands of others of somewhat lesser renown. Exile in London and Cap d'Antibes waited in the wings, but not for long.

Over the coming years, Berezovsky would spend much of his time plotting and rethinking his situation, often at Château de la Garoupe. No doubt whilst there, he would have reflected on how matters had quickly turned so sour. The journalist, Yevgeny Kiselyov, reflected on how, when he had interviewed him in the past, he (Berezovsky) had greatly appreciated his grand estate on

Cap d'Antibes. Unlike his fellow oligarchs and business associates, some of whom would later purchase properties on Cap d'Antibes, he apparently did not seek to lavishly update the main residence or to transform the gardens. Nor, according to Kiselyov, did he mind the fact that windows at Château de la Garoupe, were 'squeaky' and that the doors were 'cracked'! As Berezovsky reportedly put it: *'The whole beauty of this house and this garden is due to their antiquity. They convey a sense of time'*. Such a stance may seem surprising, given the image generally portrayed of Russian oligarchs; but in a way, in Kiselyov's view, it bore testimony to Berezovsky's intellectual pedigree. Although regarded by many as just a ruthless operator, there was no refuting the fact that he was a widely read and thoughtful individual. As he put it, Berezovsky was *'a true European, a Ph.D. and an intellectual of the highest order with a highly developed sense of taste and manners'*.

Whatever the veracity of such personal observations, Berezovsky's life in exile, with London as his main base, continued to be mired in disputes and controversy. His business interests were also severely compromised. Having previously lost control of a major television channel was one thing; the much-hyped legal confrontation with Roman Abramovich concerning the precise structure of the ownership of the Russian energy company Gazprom Neft (formerly Sibneft) was another. Loss of that case proved to be a costly and soul-sapping affair. As if all this were not enough, on-going inquiries by French authorities into his tax affairs and into the sources of the monies used in purchasing Château de la Garoupe and other assets, seriously undermined his peace of mind. The reputed arrival by helicopter of armed investigators at Château de la Garoupe would not have pleased the oligarch. The invading force most certainly discombobulated his elderly mother who was quietly resting up in the residence. She was presumably hoping for a quiet life away from it all, and undoubtedly wanting for nothing. But the fallout from the whole saga was not to end there. In March 2013 Berezovsky was found dead at his estate – Titness Park, near

Ascot, Berkshire. He was 67 years of age. Needless to say, his passing raised numerous questions as to whether or not third parties were involved. For want of sufficiently incriminating evidence, the coroner had no choice but to record an open verdict.

(ii) Roman Abramovich and Château de la Croë

Given the nature of their bitter relationship, it is ironic that Roman Abramovich should have earlier come to own a substantial estate very close to Château de la Garoupe. He purchased Château de la Croë in 2001. Classical in style, it had been built in 1927 for the newspaper magnate, Sir William Pomeroy Burton. Whilst work continued on his new residence, Sir William stayed at his villa on Cap Martin – Villa Augusta (later renamed Villa Barbara). That particular residence had previously been in the ownership of the aforementioned Prince Danilo of Montenegro. It would be interesting to know if he ever called in on Sir Pomeroy, when visiting Cap d'Antibes to meet up with his two sisters, Anastasia and Militza. The reader will be recall that, fortuitously, they happened to live close-by.

A particularly noteworthy event in the history of Abramovich's residence was the leasing of Château de la Croë, for a period of 10 years, by Edward, Duke of Windsor and his spouse, formerly Mrs Wallis Simpson. Here, behind high walls, the couple sought a degree of solace following Edward's momentous and seriously divisive decision in 1936 to renounce his position as King Edward VIII. The estate covered some 5 hectares and occupied a prime coastal site. The building had three floors, with its exterior painted white. Green shutters served to give the edifice a regal touch. Now titled the Duke and Duchess of Windsor, they immediately set about a wholesale refurbishment of the interior. By all accounts, they did so exquisitely, and expensively. Prized items and mementoes were transferred from London, in particular from Fort Belvedere and York House, the duke's former homes. To mention but a very few, they included a grand Steinway piano, books for a newly constituted library, quality pieces of furniture, together with a portrait of his mother, Queen Mary. Throughout, the royal colours – red, white and gold – predominated. Meticulous care was also taken to ensure that personal insignias (WE) adorned towels, linen in variety, writing paper, and other domestic items. To add a further touch of distinction, a personal banner was unfurled on the château's rooftop whenever they were in residence. It went without saying that, at all times, visitors of whatever standing or celebrity, were expected to show due deference and to respect protocol. Curtsying on meeting the Duchess by those fortunate enough to receive invitations to the sanctum was a *sine qua non*. The same decorum also applied even when the couple were away from Château de la Croë, and even when attending the most informal of occasions beyond their estate. To add quirky variety to the scene, Edward would often be heard blowing his adored bagpipes, whilst sporting one or other of his favourite kilts. As a particularly close friend reported, he did so '*robustly*' and '*with unaffected enjoyment*'. For the Duke of Windsor it would undoubtedly have served as a reminder of less fraught times once spent, '*en famille*', in Scotland at Balmoral.

Inevitably, the duke and duchess were frequently invited to attend dinners and soirées by the owners of other palatial residences across the Côte d'Azur. As honoured guests, their mere presence would ensure considerable cachet both for their hosts and for other invitees. Given their proximity, the couple would occasionally pay visits both to Villa Eilenroc and the Grand Hôtel du Cap. It also goes without saying that the royals entertained majestically at La Croë. Figuring among those welcomed were the British Prime Minister, Lloyd George, together with his wife, Margaret. At the time, they were celebrating their 50th wedding anniversary on the Côte d'Azur. Winston Churchill and his spouse Clementine were also among the great and the good who were invited to enter the royal domain. Another notable guest was the writer Somerset Maugham.

The duke and duchess, suitably attired (*noblesse oblige*), were also to be seen at parties and dinners held at Maxime Elliot's famed

Château de l'Horizon in nearby Golfe-Juan. Modernist in style and designed by the celebrated architect Barry Dierks, the château was a place in which those of somewhat lesser fame or substance would frequently gather. Winston Churchill was again a frequent and pampered guest. In the mornings, the former Prime Minister religiously devoted time to writing in bed, with cigar dangerously to the fore. After lunch, he could be seen sliding bulbously into the swimming pool carved, like Eden-Roc, out of the coastal rocks below. Then everything changed for all concerned.

Following the onset of the Second World War, in September 1939, the Windsors were begrudgingly obliged to pack their bags, and take leave of their much-loved palace. In 1945, following the cessation of hostilities, they returned to see what state the château was in, and to endeavour to rebuild their lives there. According to one report the damage incurred to La Croë was minimal, with just a few windows shattered and some trees cut down. But later, in a letter to Alexandra Metcalfe (née Curzon, and known to her friends as 'Baba') the duchess claimed that the frame and interior of the château had indeed been severely affected. Thus, in February 1945, she wrote:

> 'La Croë has been occupied by the Italians and the Germans, has been shelled from the sea by us and last but not least ruined by the Germans. The Americans are now dealing with the latter and we ought to be able to have our representatives inside the gate shortly'.

With personal and political circumstances rapidly changing, in August 1948 the Windsors reluctantly decided to pick up sticks and leave their much-loved retreat for good. An almost surreal phase in the history of the villa, and of Cap d'Antibes, had come to an abrupt end. In 1950/51, Aristotle Onassis bought the residence, and remained its owner until 1957. Thereafter, his brother-in-law and business rival, Stavros Niarchos, acquired the *'domaine'*. He too was a renowned and very wealthy Greek shipping magnate.

Château de la Croë

Following his brief period of ownership, the villa was apparently left virtually abandoned, taken over by squatters and damaged by fires. Despite this, with its extensive grounds and its stunning outlook, in the right hands it was most certainly worthy of careful renovation – albeit at a price.

The hands concerned would turn out to be those of another high-profile oligarch – Roman Abramovich. Following its purchase, he set about the wholescale renovation of the château, together with a re-landscaping of its grounds. Although details are limited, it can be assumed that nothing would be spared in styling and furnishing the interior. By 2008 major works were seemingly complete, although there was always something luxurious to be added (e.g. a roof-top, ecological swimming pool). Needless to say, as on his yacht, a plethora of security and surveillance systems were of the highest technological order (see below). Maybe so, but even the wealthiest of the wealthy cannot be assured of protecting themselves from all outside events, especially those of a wider political and fiscal nature. Even for an oligarch some things just cannot be controlled, as future political developments would soon make clear.

Finally, as was the case with Beresovsky, the level of investment involved in the purchase and refurbishment of La Croë became subject to investigation by the French authorities. Yet again, they were keen to ensure that associated wealth tax obligations had been fully met and that money laundering was at no time involved. In this regard, in September 2018 the Court of Cassation in Paris adjudged that in his returns Abramovich had allowed his estate to be seriously undervalued. *In toto*, Château de la Croë was, in its estimation, worth the equivalent of 87 million euros; twice that said to be submitted for tax assessment. By all accounts, Abramovich's representatives apparently queried the way in which the evaluation had been determined (by comparing Château de la Croë with similarly prestigious properties on Cap Ferrat and Cap d'Ail), but seemingly to no avail. Perhaps the only saving grace, at least as far as Abramovich's self-esteem was concerned, was that an architect's report prepared for the authorities concerned, claimed that, in '*its level of luxury and elegance*', the property was a jewel, '*sans pareil*' on the Côte d'Azur. As to the size of penalties eventually incurred, they are said to have amounted to a princely 1.2 million euros: small beer for an oligarch. But as is often the case with such matters, much of the detail is lost in a cloud of public unknowing. Ironically, Abramovich's château lies within a mere stone's throw of the *Anse de Faux Argent* (Cove of Counterfeit Money) and the *Baie des Milliardaires* (Billionaires Bay).

Perhaps not unexpectedly, some of the proposed developments at the villa also faced local scrutiny. One particular controversy that gained much publicity at the time was the desire on the part of Abramovich to build a jetty (small harbour) out into the sea immediately below the château. With such a fixture in place, those arriving, presumably aboard private yachts or other luxurious craft, would not be unduly inconvenienced. For Abramovich it would have been a grandiose way in which to receive honoured guests. But for locals it was a development much too far. Fittingly, the fight to stop the submission began with a seemingly innocuous complaint lodged by a local fisherman. But what was to follow, in terms of the strength of local opposition to the planning application, was to exceed all expectations. The application was duly dismissed out of hand.

Whilst Château Croë was the jewel in Abramovich's crown, perhaps just as self-affirming, were the superyachts that he owned. Over the years, such was his desire to remain ahead of the game, that he frequently sold them on, only to replace them with even larger, technologically superior and impressively designed vessels; again with no expense spared. Those that were deemed to be passé were quickly substituted: Ecstasea, Pelorus and Luna being cases in point. But not, as yet, his other yachts, Eclipse and Solaris (but see

Eclipse – off Antibes

later). At one stage Eclipse was the largest in the world. Just over 163 metres in length, its superfluity of high-tech features includes a dedicated missile detection system and a submarine, should, for whatever reason, a speedy retreat be called for. According to some sources, this vessel cost its owner an estimated 340 million euros, and is currently deemed to be the second largest in the world. As for the technologically advanced motor yacht Solaris, it is nearly 140 metres long. Although seen offshore only occasionally, Antibes inevitably gained some kudos from the association.

In January 2023 Abramovich was thought by the Forbes real-time list to have a net worth of nearly $8.7 billion dollars. Amazingly, despite the enormity of this latter estimate, and his high international profile, it only placed him in twelfth place in the list of Russian oligarchs, and 226th globally. What his ranking is at the time of writing it is impossible to say. Much has happened in the meantime.

(iii) The Suleyman Kerimov Affair

In November 2017, French fiscal authorities launched yet another investigation into the ownership, value and manner of purchase of a suite of villas located close by Château de la Croë, Villa Eilenroc and the grounds the Hôtel du Cap-Eden-Roc. Each of the properties, which included villas Hier, Medy Roc, Lexa and Fiorella, formed a virtually contiguous block of outstanding real estate. According to official records, they were all deemed to be in the ownership of a Swiss financier, named Alexander Studhalter. Given the hefty sums undoubtedly involved, however, suspicions were inevitably aroused; the feeling being that Studhalter was simply acting as a front for the real owner. At one stage it was thought that Corsican speculators might have been nefariously implicated. But, following a raid on the said properties, attention shifted to the Russian oligarch, Suleyman Kerimov – a former deputy from Dagestan and a member of the Federation Council of Russia. From very lowly beginnings, like Abramovich, he had built up a vast and varied fortune through arcane dealings in oil, gold and banking, to name but a few. As for Studhalter, he was known to be a close financial confidant of Kerimov. The maze of financial arrangements that underpinned the whole process of purchase, together with associated business structures involving differing companies, banks and shareholders was mind-bogglingly complex.

No doubt the high-paced and high-spending life of Kerimov while on the Riviera – one that climaxed publicly in a dramatic fireball of a crash in his Ferrari Enzo on the Promenade des Anglais in Nice – fed into the concerns that the authorities had regarding the structure of his business affairs. So too did the fact that some of his many very high-end sports cars were found to be housed in one or other of the villas concerned, and that Kerimov and his family were said to be frequently in residence there. No doubt surprisingly to some, despite detailed investigations and much supporting evidence, in May 2018 all charges were formally dropped, not only against Kerimov, but also his Swiss associate. Studhalter was accepted as owner of the set of villas, which were then putatively assessed to have a total valuation of 300 million euros.

Yet another contentious imbroglio in which Kerimov became doubtfully involved concerned a small but highly prized promontory at the southern tip of Cap d'Antibes. In an interview with one journalist, he pronounced that he was in fact the owner of this particular area of land, or at least part of it. Pointe de l'Ilette by name, it is located due south of the Grand Hôtel-Eden-Roc and directly opposite Villa Eilenroc. It had long caught the covetous eyes of those keen to establish villas there. The fact that it looked out upon an open seascape, and was relatively private, simply added to the attractiveness of the site, as did the presence of a small private harbour.

Over the years, portions of this tract came into the, often contentious, ownership of a whole series of individuals, far too numerous to detail here. However, *en passant*, it is worth making reference to a dramatically eye-catching residence that once dominated the landscape – Villa de la Mosquée. Built in the latter part of the 19th century and Moorish in style, it was a singular feature of the landscape, and attracted the interest of artists (for example Matisse) and photographers, as well as the public at large. Following its demolition, a small number of other villas were built on the promontory, but they were inevitably much less exotic. All that now remains of the said villa's presence is the name of the roadway that penetrates into the heart of the promontory – Chemin de la Mosquée. As it happens, tortuous disputes have dogged the little strip of land. Kerimov's half-hearted intervention was but one of many, and would seem not to have been pursued any further.

According to the Forbes listings for 2022 Kerimov was estimated to be the 21st richest of the Russian oligarchs, and was ranked 148th globally. His wealth is thought to be around $12.4 billion. Whilst Kerimov's business affairs and behaviour have attracted publicity, it is worth recognising the charitable work he has engaged in

Villa de la Mosquée (Mauresque)

Amadea

through the Kerimov Foundation. But as to whether or not this compensated for all that had gone before is an open question.

Like many of the Russian oligarchs, Kerimov owns a superyacht. Named 'Amadea', and at 106 metres long, it is said to have cost $300 million.

(iv) Andrey Melnichenko and Villa Altaïr

Of the clutch of oligarchs associated with properties on Cap d'Antibes, at least up until more recently, another who has become mired in controversy is Andrey Melnichenko. He, together with his Serbian wife (a former model and pop singer), had a new villa built at a site abutting Berezovsky's former estate, and overlooking the Baie de la Garoupe – Villa Altaïr. Unlike Berezovsky and Abramovich, however, Melnichenko seemingly played no part in the privatizations that took place during Yeltsin's period in office. He had only recently graduated from Moscow State University where he had studied physics. Having achieved further qualifications in the field of finance, he was, however, in a position to take full and speedy advantage of the more open economic climate that then prevailed. His fortune was built up over a number of years and began with the establishment of a private bank. Astute and dynamic, he quickly moved on to become a major shareholder in various enterprises involving coal-mining, specialized steel production, chemicals (especially fertilizers) and electricity generation.

Although generally maintaining a lower profile, his extravagant wedding party at Villa Altaïr in 2005 was widely reported upon, with particular interest being shown in the impressive list of celebrated guests. They included eminent politicians and entrepreneurs, as well as celebrities from the world of international entertainment. Given his background in science and interest in technology, it is hardly surprising that Melnichenko should have had a hands-on involvement in the design and construction of his two state-of-the-art superyachts – M/Y A (2008) and S/Y A (2017). Both vessels would regularly be seen skirting the coastal fringes of Cap d'Antibes, and turning heads in so doing.

He may have arrived late on the plutocratic stage but in 2023 Melnichenko was deemed to have a net worth of $27.1 billion.

Motor Yacht A

Sailing Yacht A

Dilbar

According to Forbes, this placed him 8th on the list of Russians, and 50th world-wide.

Finally, it is worth making reference to what is reputed to be the heaviest all the superyachts – Dilbar. Owned by the oligarch Alisher Usmanov, and 156 metres in length, it was frequently to be seen occupying the top berth in the harbour at Antibes. According to the Forbes ratings he was worth $14.7 billion, ranking 121st in the world.

An Uncertain Future

Despite the enormity of the figures cited above, the assets of oligarchs, and of other very wealthy Russians, have more recently come under far more serious pressure, following the decision taken by President Putin to invade Ukraine in February, 2022. In response, a powerful body of European countries, together with the USA and others, have since joined forces to impose severe sanctions on individuals and companies. The sealing-off of markets, the withdrawal of major international businesses from Russia itself, the closure of access to financial, legal and insurance services, strict limitations on travel and use of airspace are but a few of the measures taken to demonstrate the strength of feeling towards the gratuitous invasion of Ukraine. At the time of writing, such measures, together with the supply of military hardware and strategic information, have helped to support the Ukrainian fight-back, but at this stage the future for all concerned remains perilously uncertain.

All of this has been effected in the hope that Putin will rethink the situation; one that is evidently having a negative effect on the Russian domestic economy and, most certainly, on Russia's international standing. Longer-term, future diplomatic relations worldwide will surely be severely compromised. However, there has been a *'quid pro quo'*, with countervailing measures taken by Russia, most notably in regard to the export of oil and gas. Loss of grain and other agricultural goods from Ukraine itself has also become an issue of major global consequence and concern. Putin's threat of nuclear retaliation has upped the ante, and to an alarming degree.

These developments clearly demonstrate how quickly fortunes, both literal and metaphorical, can change as a result of events globally. As far as the whole of the Côte d'Azur is concerned, the situation has already had a significant impact. Personal sanctions and the freezing of associated assets have forced or obliged Russians, and not just those of considerable wealth, to pick up sticks and to move on. Although it is far from being the most significant factor, their departure must surely have had a material impact on the high-end property market. The virtual disappearance of the Russian language from billboards and in the promotional literature of estate agents bears some superficial testimony to the changes taking place. This would certainly seem to be the case as far as Cap d'Antibes is concerned. On a wider front, but one of wholly minor consequence in the scheme of things, marinas, esteemed restaurants, casinos, nightclubs across the Riviera must have been caught up in the swirling backwash.

In the midst of it all, one very specific issue that has figured prominently in the media, and one that is perhaps of marginal impact as far as Antibes and its marina are concerned, is the effort being made by authorities world-wide to track down and commandeer superyachts, given the sanctions being imposed on oligarchs and others of great wealth. Across the globe a cat and mouse game continues to be played out. Of the yachts currently in the limelight, a number of those mentioned above have figured most prominently.

Given the dangers of sequestration, major efforts have been made to escape the authorities. Thus, in April 2022 the 140 metre superyacht owned by Abramovich – Solaris – was berthed at the port of Bodrum in south-west Turkey, having departed in a hurry from Barcelona. It first headed to the port of Tivat in Montenegro, and then on to Bodrum. Here, it was hoped that a safe haven would be secured. Yet another of the oligarch's vessels – Eclipse – is said to have tied up at another Turkish port, that of Marmaris. Of particular relevance here is the fact that, for much broader reasons, both Turkey and Montenegro have, at the time of writing, chosen not to impose sanctions on Russians or their yachts. Political and business relations with Russia are more important to them. There is little need to wonder what the late King Nicholas of Montenegro would have thought of it all. Not much one would surmise, given his family's particularly close ties with the Romanovs.

It will be recalled that the oligarch Suleiman Kerimov has been at the centre of a series of controversies pertaining to the ownership of some key properties on Cap d'Antibes. Whilst those charges were eventually dismissed, he too has now had to face the problem of being sanctioned, in this case by the U.S. Treasury Department. As if previous accusations were not enough, his superyacht, the Amadea, was seized by the Fijian Government, and handed over to American authorities. Interestingly, in a report in The Times (10 December, 2022) reference is specifically made to the seizure of the yacht. It was said to have *'a helipad, a swimming pool, spacious accommodation for 16 guests, and all the other amenities required by a Russian oligarch'*. This in itself is not particularly remarkable. What *is* of interest, however, is that the authorities concerned also discovered on–board the yacht what was thought be a genuine Fabergé egg. As previously noted, the imperial yacht – Standart – also carried such an egg; one that had been specifically commissioned by the Imperial family. As it turned out, the egg on the Amadea was deemed by experts not to be a genuine Fabergé, albeit one of very high value in its own right.

Andrei Melnichenko has likewise been subject to sanctions. At the time of writing, he remains the owner of his superyachts, but for how long is again uncertain. SY A (Sailing Yacht A) has seemingly been seized in the port of Trieste. Dilbar, the superyacht owned by Alisher Usmanov, is also under surveillance and, at the time of writing, is apparently berthed in Hamburg undergoing repairs. But, world-wide, the chase goes on.

Whatever the future might hold for particular oligarchs, there is no gainsaying that at all social levels the Russian presence throughout the Riviera has, to use an appropriate metaphor, been holed below the waterline. As to the future, all will clearly depend on unpredictable political events and how they eventually unfold. What is certain, however, is that another remarkable chapter in the history of the Côte d'Azur has been written; and most certainly in that of Cap d'Antibes, Antibes and Juan-les-Pins.

Résumé

By way of summary, through a suite of five discrete essays, the central aim of this short and highly selective study has been to introduce the reader to just some of the more notable personalities, families and associated properties that have figured in shaping the history and development of Cap d'Antibes and its two adjoining towns – Antibes and Juan-les-Pins. Of those concerned, the great majority arrived in the area from outside: some by accident, others by design. Whilst this is the case, in no way is it meant to assume that the roles played by locals have been of inconsequence. This is most certainly not the case. They are the bedrock on which all else has rested. It is those from within, together with those from afar, who have jointly succeeded in making the region such a fascinating and exceptional place.

Notes

1 Antibes and Juan-les-Pins

1. Depigny, J.P. *'Antibes – Ancien et Moderne'*, Gustave Gratiot, Paris, 1849.
2. King,Ross. *'The Judgement of Paris'*, Pimlico, 2007, p235
3. Dempster, C. *'The Maritime Alps and their seabord'*, 1885.
4. Scott, William. *'The Riviera'*, A&C Black, London, 1907.
5. Hare, Augustus. *'The Riviera'*, George Allan and Unwin, London, 1896.
6. Château de la Garoupe would later gain questionable renown as the home of the Russian oligarch – Boris Beresovsky (see 5).
7. Picasso had first established the tentative beginnings of a relationship with the Russian ballerina Olga Kokhlova in Paris in May 1917. As a member of Diaghilev's company, she was performing in the ballet *'Parade'*, for which Picasso had been contracted to assist in the design of costumes and stage sets. Unwilling to commit herself whole-heartedly at the outset, she eventually succumbed to his persistent expressions of affection. In July 1918 the couple were married in the Russian Cathedral in Paris.
8. Richardson, J, *'A Life of Picasso. Volume III, The Triumphant Years'*, p163.
9. Richardson, op.cit, p159.
10. The relationship staggered on, but in the end Olga decided to call it a day. Interestingly, she chose to establish a new life for herself in Cannes. It was there in 1934 that she passed away, aged 64. To her dying day she remained Picasso's wife – at least on paper. In a final twist, Picasso would breathe his last in the hill village of Mougins, just a few kilometres away from the *Cimitière du Grand Jas* in Cannes where she had been laid to rest.
11. Vaill, Amanda, *'Everybody Was So Young Then'*, Little, Brown and Company, 1998, p163.
12. In 2006 the owners of the hotel (still members of the Estène family) acquired Hôtel Juana.
13. Sometimes Florence's maiden name was aristocratically styled as La Caze; at others simply Lacase.
14. The villa, named 'Semiramis', after a mythical Babylonian/Assyrian queen, was set in extensive landscaped grounds. It was built in 1884 and was

originally called Château Saint-Roche. The Goulds made very limited use of the residence, but their wealth being what it was, it was hardly considered a matter of any major consequence.

15   In time it would gain international recognition for its association with the Fitzgeralds, as well as its Art Deco refurbishment.
16   In 2006 Hôtel Juana was bought by the Estène family.
17   Florence Gould died without heirs. Most of her estate was directed to the Florence J. Gould Foundation, which she established following her husband's death in 1956. Its remit was to promote French-American friendship. Over the years Florence established literary prizes and sponsored museums and art galleries (e.g. the Metropolitan Museum of Art in New York).

2   Villa Eilenroc

1   Sometimes referred to as a *récit de voyage'*, '*Sur l'eau*' was first published in 1888. Rather than a precise chronological diary, it is essentially a summary of reflections and experiences gleaned during his many stays in the area between 1881 and 1887. There have been a number of English versions, the most recent being 'Afloat', translated by Mario Johnston, Peter Owen, London, 1995.

2   In comparative reference to the elegant neo-classical château, completed in 1765 during the reign of Louis XV of France in the grounds of the Estate of Trianon at Versailles. It would later become known as *'Le Petit Trianon'*, and was famously used as a favoured retreat by Marie Antoinette.

3   For an overview, see Gayraud, D. *'Eilenroc, une domaine d'exception'*, Nice Historique, Volume 420, 105-111, 2009.

4   Montrose, James Wyllie's birthplace, is located just 20 miles from Tannadice, the small settlement that was home to Alexander Loudon. Whether the families knew each other and whether or not this was how James Wyllie found about Eilenroc being for sale is seemingly not known.

5   John Gladstone moved to Liverpool in 1786 and began trading initially in grain. But his business soon widened out considerably, particularly after a number of his brothers had joined him. Over the years he built a considerable fortune; most questionably through his ownership of sugar plantations worked by slaves and, later, indentured labourers. Following the ending of the East India Company's monopoly in 1814, he began trading in India, with Calcutta serving as a base. It was in regard to the latter that he joined forces with James Wyllie. One of his sons was William Ewart Gladstone. On four separate occasions between 1868 and 1894 he served as Prime Minister of the United Kingdom.

6   Wyllie became a highly regarded benefactor to the town of Antibes; so

Notes

much so that in recognition of his charitable endowments a shore-hugging boulevard edging of the Cap was later named after him.

7   In her guide, entitled *'Cannes and its Surroundings'*, published in1914, Amy Benecke notes that, after having lunched at the Grand Hôtel du Cap, '...at two o'clock on Tuesdays or Fridays, Mr Wyllie's charming garden, Eilenroc, can be visited. The carriages drive up to the gate, where an entrance fee of one franc per person is asked; then a short walk up the carriage drive leads to the garden, which is well kept and arranged with little paths running down to the sea in many places.'
8   Retrieved from : http//www.vitber.com/eng/lot/20342.
9   Comments attached in the following: https://www.npg.org.uk/collections/search/person/mp102804/sir-coleridge-arthur-fitzroy-kennard-1st-bt. Retrieved 9-7-20.
10 Porter, J. *'Yoï. The Remarkable Life of Cornelia Crosse'*, Matador, 2018.
11 In Rome, Yoï met and married the sculptor, Antonio Maraini. She herself became a successful writer, firstly under the name Yoï Pawlowska (her mother's name) and then Yoï Maraini. The couple had two children – Fsco and Grabo.
12 Grant Richards, *'The Coast of Pleasure'*, 1928, Harper &Brothers, p122
13 Highly erotic (homoerotic) in parts, some have suggested it is a spoof publication, designed to denigrate Kennard or simply to amuse.
14 For a detailed account of Jacques Lebaudy's life, see *'L'Empereur du Sahara'*, Phillipe di Folco, Gallade Editions, 2014.
15 The couple had a child in 1933 – Sadruddin. He would spend many happy times at their villa. Following their divorce in 1943, Jane Andrée used the residence as a base for another 40 or so years. It was while in Antibes, in 1976, that she died, at the age of 78. She was laid to rest at her home in Chambéry. Her former husband had passed away in 1957. Thereafter, their villa was abandoned, subject to damage and used by squatters. Formally designated as an architectural feature of significance it has since been expensively, and extensively, renovated, but with due cognizance of its earlier Islamic associations and distinctive features.
16 To avoid confiscation during the German Occupation, these and other paintings owned by the Beaumonts were spirited out of France. In 1948, the Louis Dudley Foundation donated a number to the Cleveland Museum of Art.

3   Villa Soleil, Grand Hôtel du Cap and Château des Enfants

1   Duquesnel, F. *'Souvenirs Littéraires'*, Librairie Plon, 1922.
2   Hillier Onslow was born in 1853 and became the 4th Earl Onslow, at the age

of 17. His stately home and estate was that of Clandon Park. A Conservative Member of Parliament, he held various Offices of State, and between 1898 and 1892 served as 11th Governor of New Zealand. Lord Onslow died in 1911, aged 58.

For details, see: http://www.force-one.net/hotel-du-cap-eden-roc-a-legendary-150-years.

3 Not that Eastman was unsympathetic, for he too was a major philanthropist.
4 Morris, M. *'My Life in Movement'*, Peter Owen, 1969. Reprint – The International of MMM Ltd, 2003.
5 Fergusson was initially drawn to Impressionism, but later displayed an interest in Fauvism. In due course he would be classed as a key figure among what is referred to as the 'Scottish Colourists' school. See: Emerson, R. *'The Architect and the Dancer'*, Charles Rennie Mackintosh Sociery, Volume 98, Spring 2014.
6 Richardson, J. *'A Life of Picasso. Volume III The Triumphant Years 1917-1932'*, Pimlico, 2009, p234.
7 Interestingly, he claimed to be a distant relative of the Eastman who established the Kodak Company.
8 Eastman, M. *'Leon Trotsky:The Portrait of a Youth'*, Faber and Gwyer, 1926.
9 Max had previously been married to a radical socialist and early feminist named Ida Rauh. They had divorced in 1922.
10 Irmscher, C. *'Max Eastman. A Life'*, Yale University Press. 2017. See also, William, L. O' Neill, *'The Last Romantic. A Life of Max Eastman'*, Oxford University Press, 1978.
11 The couple set up home in Martha's Vineyard. It was there that Eliena furthered her interests in drawing and in writing poetry. Fittingly, a major joint project involved the translation of Trotsky's *'History of the Russian Revolution'* into English. Eliena died in 1959, whilst Max, who had by then abandoned his radical leftist views, moved to Barbados. It was there that he passed away in 1969, aged 86 – the end of a tumultuous but truly productive life.
12 Following the outbreak of the Second World War, Margaret moved to Glasgow. Over the coming years she developed a notation system for dance, and continued to further her interest in education through dance and the performing arts. She also spent more time writing and developing her undoubted skills as a painter. She died in 1980, aged 89.
13 Murphy, M.C. *'M.Sella, Hotel proprietor is a social philosopher.'* Life Magazine, September 1948.

Notes

4   Russians and Montenegrins in Residence

1   Paul Alexandrovich Stroganov led an interesting life. Resident in Paris during the French Revolution, he immersed himself in the upheavals, engaged in radical discourse and even joined the Jacobite Club. Singularly unimpressed, Empress Catherine II ordered him home, and then banished him to the family estate near Moscow. Welcomed back into the courtly fold by Tsar Paul I, he renewed his longstanding friendship with his son, the future Tsar Alexander I, with whom he felt free to explore the prospects of political reform in Russia; that is until the tsar shifted his ideological stance to a more conservative agenda. Paul Alexandrovich held positions of high government office, and later joined the military, fighting with distinction in the Napoleonic Wars. He died in 1817.

2   In Antibes, Fersen is duly recognized, for he has had both a street and a Collège named after him.

3   Interestingly, both he and his brother were sojourning in Cannes, together with their father – Grand Duke Nicholas Nikolaevich in 1881, when they heard the dramatic news of Tsar Alexander II's assassination back in St Petersburg. At that time, Nicholas was 25 years old, his brother 17. As it happened, that very same year their mother, Grand Duchess Alexandra Petrovna (formerly Princess Alexandra of Oldenburg) decided to leave her husband, but refused to agree to a divorce. It had been a disastrous relationship from the outset, but his philandering and, in particular, his open relationship with a former dancer, Catherine Chislova, proved just too much bear. Following Chislova's death Nicholas slowly lost his mind. Declared insane, he spent his final days locked away in a home on the Crimea in 1891. That year, a vast palace in St Petersburg had been gifted to him by his father Nicholas I. Called the Nickolovsky or Nicholas Palace, it subsequently reverted to the Crown, to cover for the debts that the Grand Duke had accumulated in mortgaging the property. The palace later housed the Xenia Institute for Noble Young Ladies. More prosaically, under the Bolsheviks, it became the Palace of Labour.

4   Representing the tsar, Grand Duke Nicholas attended the celebrations that were held in the Montenegrin capital – Cetinje – to mark the fiftieth anniversary of his father-in-law's reign. It was then that Prince Nikolai pronounced himself King. He must have been delighted on that occasion to be elevated to the position of field marshal in the Russian army. The beauty of the landscape overwhelmed Nicholas. He claimed that it rivalled even the Caucasus, in terms of natural splendour, if not grandiosity.

5   It will be recalled that Jacques Lebaudy sought to acquire a portion of his kingdom to set up his own fiefdom (See 2).

6   The eldest daughter, Princess Zorka (1864-1890), had married Crown Prince

Peter Karadordevic, later King Peter of Serbia, in 1883. The couple had 6 children. Zorka died aged just 26.

7 George was the youngest of seven children born to Tsar Alexander II's sister, Maria Nicolaevna. He became the 6th Duke of Leuchtenberg in 1901. The marriage, which had produced two children, failed.

8 Following the October Revolution, Alexander Georgevich made strenuous efforts to ensure the safety of Tsar Nicholas II and his family, including a visit to Berlin to enlist the help of the German Emperor, Wilhelm II.

9 Yousoupov was closely involved in the murder of Rasputin. It was carried out in his family's palace in December 1916.

10 Houston, M. *'Nikola and Milena: King and Queen of the Black Mountain'*, 2003

11 The epithet 'black' was purportedly used to refer to their dark hair and swarthy complexions – a reflection of their Balkan origins. But there was surely more to it than that. Ironically, the sisters were from a country whose name signified 'The Black Mountain'.

12 Nadejda had previously been engaged to Prince Oleg Constantinovich. He died in action, soon after the outbreak of the Great War in Lithuania.

13 Radzinsky, Edvard: *'Rasputin. The Last Word'*, Weidenfeld and Nicholson, 2000, p 356.

14 Orlov died in Paris in 1927, aged 58. He was buried not far from Fontainebleau in the Cimetière de Samois-sur-Seine.

15 The Germans moved into the Crimea following the Treaty of Brest-Litovsk (20 February/3 March). The Treaty meant that Russia was no longer involved in the First World War. They would soon be obliged to leave the Crimea, however, as Red Army forces moved in to take over. But before so doing, the Romanov party was offered sanctuary in Germany. The offer was refused.

16 Prinz Roman Romanov, *'Am Hof des letzten Zaren 1896-1919'*, Piper, München, 1997, p 437.

17 Before her marriage, and much to her mother's immense chagrin, she converted to Catholicism, having been raised in Eastern Orthodoxy. So hurt was her mother, that she refused to attend the wedding.

18 At the end of the Second World War, Elena joined her husband in exile in Egypt. She died in Montpellier in 1952.

19 In addition to the grand dukes and their wives, the party included: Anastasia's two children by her first marriage, Sergei and Helen, plus Helen's husband – Count Stephan Tyszkiewcz. The children of Grand Duke Peter and Grand Duchess Militza: Prince Roman Petrovich; Princess Marina Petrovna; Princess Nadejda Petrovna Orlov, her husband Prince Nicholas, and their daughter Princess Irina Orlov.

Notes

20. Duchess Jutta of Mecklenburg-Streliz married Crown Prince Danilo of Montenegro in 1899, after converting to Eastern Orthodoxy from the Lutheran faith. On her marriage, and according to Montenegrin custom, she took the name Militza. She joined her husband in exile in 1916. Milena became Queen of Montenegro in 1921, albeit for just a week, following her husband's bizarre decision to abdicate the throne. They lived in exile in France, but following his death in 1939, she moved to Rome, joining her sister–in-law, Queen Elena of Italy. Jutta remained in Rome, until her death in 1946, aged 66.
21. Houston, M, *'Nikola and Milena: King and Queen of the Black Mountain'*, 2003, p347.
22. In 1989 the remains of ex-king Nikola of Montenegro and his wife were transferred back to Montenegro, where a dedicated family chapel had been constructed for her at Cetinje.
23. Château Thénard was built in 1865 for Baron Thénard. He was a highly honoured chemist from a humble farming background. The inventor of such products as blue cobalt, hydrogen peroxide and bromine, he became very wealthy. His villa was built near that of his close friend, the highly celebrated algologist and plantsman – Gustave Thuret.
24. Nicholas and his wife would not be alive to witness it, but they would most certainly have been impressed with the establishment nearby, in 1948, of the famed *La Roseraie Meilland*. Over the years members of the family were responsible for the breeding of numerous new varieties of roses – most notably that of the hybrid tea cultivar labelled 'Peace' (for sale in the English-speaking world) – in its original French form 'Madame Antoine Meilland'. Two other flower businesses operating in the locality were Barberet and Kriloff.
25. Besse, Jean-Paul, *'Le grand-duc Nicholas, tsar ou régent?*, Via Romana, 2018.
26. Interestingly, of the boys, Nikolai ended up marrying Irina, the only daughter of Felix Yousoupov and his wife, also named Irina. She was the daughter of Tsar Nicholas II's sister Grand Duchess Xenia and her husband, Grand Duke Alexander.
27. Until he was 10 years of age, Dimitri was educated locally, with a strong emphasis being placed on the teaching of Russian traditions. The family then moved on to Italy. With them there were Prascovia's parents. No doubt, while there, the group would have met up with Elena – Queen of Italy – in Rome. Later, following his death, Grand Duke Peter's wife Militza joined them.
28. Golitsyn was prime minister for a number of months during the unrest that turned into the February Revolution. He accepted the establishment of the First Duma and tried to persuade the Tsar that it should not be prorogued. Despite this, however, during the February Revolution he was confined to the

Peter and Paul Fortress. Following his release he was reduced to repairing shoes and looking after public gardens. Suspected of counter-revolutionary activity, he was arrested in February, 1925 and eventually executed in July of that year.

[29] Cited in: *'Quand les Russes s'installaient en masse sur la Côte d'Azur, il y un siècle'*, Nice-Matin 14/06/2018.

[30] He would gain acclaim and notoriety in 1955 as the author of 'Lolita'.

[31] Boyd, B. *'Vladimir Nabokov. The Russian Years'*. Chatto and Windus, 1990, p 488.

[32] The matter is difficult to resolve purely from this source. It is, however, worth noting that Sergei only became the 8th Duke in 1942, following the death of his stepbrother Alexander. It is possible that Alexander was the owner, but it is not certain where he was based after having taken his leave of Russia. He was certainly in France when he died, but based far away in the Pyrénées region.

[33] Interestingly, it was to the same place in 1781 that one of Empress Catherine the Great's lovers – Grigori Orlov – accompanied his young wife, Princess Catherine Orlovna (née Zinovyevna), as she vainly sought a cure for tuberculosis.

5 Oligarchs: Rise and Retreat

[1] A rash of hurried urban developments in the sixties and seventies significantly disfigured the landscape in numerous interstitial parts of the Riviera, as efforts were made to accommodate a growing and wider social spectrum of visitors, as well as an expanding resident population in urgent need of cheaper housing. Unsurprisingly, many commentators have spoken of the 'assassination' and 'uglification' of the Côte d'Azur, and the brutal 'triumph of concrete'.

[2] Aubry,B. *'Les Milliardaires de la Côte'*, L'Archipel, 2010

[3] For a detailed discussion of the promontory and some its personalities, both past and present, see the previously cited 'www.ilovecapdantibes.com'.

General References

Archives Municipales. *Antibes: Cent Ans d'Expansion Urbaine, 1860-1960.* 2000
Archives Municipalaes. *Antibes: Grandeur et Servitudes d'une Place Forte.* Undated
Alpine, O. *Nice et Antibes, Capitales Azuréennes: De La Fleur Coupée.* Revue de Géographie, 1958
Antonini Basset-Terrusse, Elisabeth & Claude. *Antibes ou la Fuite Du Temps 1860- 1960.* Joie de Lire
Arrigo-Schwartz, Martine. *Âme Slave au Pays Bleu.* Éditions Serre, 2008
Arthaud, Christian & Paul, Eric L. *La Côte D'Azur des Écrivains.* Aix-en-Provence, Editions Edisud, 1999
Aubry, Bruno. *Les Milliadaires de La Côte d'Azur.* L'Archipel, 2010
Baudouin, Danielle. *L'Équipement Touristique de la Commune d'Antibes 1881-1975.* Thèse de 3e cycle, Université de Nice, 1977
Baxter, John. *French Riviera and its Artists: Art, Literature, Love and Life on the Côte D'Azur.* Museyon Guides, 2015
Bergeret, Antonin. *Du Choix d'une Station d'Hiver, et en particulier du Climat d'Antibes, Études Physiologiques, Hygiéniques et Médicales.* Baillière, J-B et fils, 1864
Bertaut, Jules. *Côte d'Azur.* Paris, Hachette, 1953
Black, Jeremy. *France and the Grand Tour.* Palgrave Macmillan, 2003
Blume, Mary. *Côte d'Azur. Inventing the French Riviera.* Thames and Hudson, 1992
Boulay, Cyrille. *La France des Romanov : de la Villégiature à l'Exil.* Librairie Académique Perrin, 2010
Bouscatel, Jean. *Le Printemps sur la Riviera.* The Lotus Magazine 5, 1914
Boyd, Brian. *Vladimir Nabokov : The Russian Years.* Princeton University Press, 1993
Boyer, Marc. *L'Invention de la Côte d'Azur. L'Hiver dans le Midi.* Éditions de l'Aube, 2002
Braincourt, M. & Servat, Henry Jean. *Hôtel du Cap Eden Roc. La Légende Éternelle de la Riviera.* Flammarion, 2022
Brunel. *Russians on the Riviera.* Nice Historique, 1952

Caigny, Fernand de. *Petite Histoire de la Cité d'Antibes*. Antibes: Boyer, 1942
Cameron, Roderick. *The Golden Riviera*. Honolulu, Editions Limited, 1984
Campbell, Alexandra. *Hôtel du Cap Eden Roc. A Timeless Legend on the French Riviera*. Flammarion, 2021
Carrière d'Encausse, Hélène. *La Russie et la France*. De Pierre le Grand à Lénine, Fayard, 2019
Cars, Jean des. *Le Train Bleu et les Grands Express de la Riviera,* Denoël, 1988
Ciais, F. & Bossard, F. *La Culture de la Rose à Antibes entre Tradition et Modernité*. Conseil Général des Alpes Maritimes, 1996
Constanty, Hélène. *Razzia sur la Riviera*. Librairie Arthème, 2015
Courcy, Anne de. *Chanel's Riviera. Life, Love and the Struggle for Survival on the Côte D'Azur. 1930-1944.* Weidenfeld & Nicolson, 2020
Danielson, A. G. *A Traveler's History of Côte D'Azur*. SDP Publishing, 2012
De la Touche, Hugues. *Impératrices sur la Riviera. Naissance d'Un Art de Vivre.* Édition Thalia, 2008
Dépigny, Jean-Pierre. *Antibes Ancien et Moderne*, 1849
Di Falco, Philippe. *L'Empereur du Sahara.* Galaade Éditions, 2014
Dor de la Souchère, Elena. *Antibes. 2500 ans d'histoire*. Maisonneuve & Larose, 2006
Duménil, Renaud. *Antibes Juan-Les-Pins. Le Temps Retrouvé*, Éditions Équinoxe, 1997
Duménil, Renaud. *Antibes, Juan-Les-Pins. Le Plaisir Deployé 1900-1960*, Éditions Équinoxe, 2002
Dussaud, P. *Antibes, Ville Royale: Histoire Politique, Économique et Sociale (1608-1789),* 1944
Ellis, Leroy. *Les Russes sur la Côte d'Azur. Éditions Serre, 1988*
Escribe, Dominique. *La Côte d'Azur. Genèse d'un Mythe*. Gilbert Vitaloni, 1988
Fray, François. *La Clientèle de l'Architecte Barry Dierks sur la Côte d'Azur.* In Situ, Revue des Patrimoines, 2012
Galéries Nationales du Grand Palais. *Méditerranée De Courbet à Matisse*. Réunion des Musées Nationaux, 2000
Gasquet, Martine. *Impératrices, Artistes et Cocottes. Les Femmes sur la Riviera à la Belle Époque.* Éditions Gilletta. nice-matin, 2013
Gasquet, Martine. *Le Temps des Garçonnes. La Côte d'Azur des Années Folles*. Éditions Gilletta. nice-matin, 2022
Girard, Xavier. *French Riviera. Living Well Was the Best Revenge*. Assouline, 2002
Hare, Augustus J. C. *The Rivieras*. London, George Allen & Unwin, 1896
Hinsdale, Guy. *The Sun, Health and Heliotherapy*. The Scientific Monthly 9, 1919

Houston, Marco. *Nikola and Milena, King and Queen of the Black Mountain: The Rise and Fall of Montenegro's Royal Family*. Leppi Publications, 2003
Howarth, Patrick. *When the Riviera Was Ours*. Routledge & Kegan Paul, 1977
Irmscher, Christoph. *Max Eastman. A Life*. Yale University Press, 2017
Joannon, Pierre. *Antibes, L'Eden Retrouvé*, La Table Ronde, 2001
Joannon, Pierre. *La Riviera de Maupassant*. Nice, Demaistre, 1997
Jones, Ted. *The French Riviera : A Literary Guide for Travellers*. I. B.Tauris & Co. Ltd,
Klein-Gousseff, Catherine. *L'Exil Russe : La Fabrique du Réfugié Apatride, 1920-1939*. Paris, CNRS, 2008
Knowles, J. *Morning in Antibes: A Novel*. Macmillan, 1962
Lavayssière, Gérard. *Le Goût d'Antibes*. Mercure de France, 2004
Leveau, Béatrice. *Les Nouveaux Visages d'Antibes* in *Loisir, Environnement et Qualité de la Vie sur la Côte d'Azur*. Les Belles Lettres. 1976
Levenstein, Harvey. *Seductive Journey : American Tourists in France. From Jefferson to the Jazz Age*. The University of Chicago Press, 1998
Leymarie, Jean. *Picasso et la Méditerranée: De Courbet à Matisse*. Paris: Réunion des Musées Nationaux, p 144-52, 2000
Liégeard, Stéphen. *La Côte d'Azur*. Editions Serre, 2003
Livry, Christiane de. *Hôtel du Cap-Eden-Roc, Cap d'Antibes*. Paris, Assouline, 2007
Lovell, Mary S. *The Riviera Set*. Abacus, 2017
Madsen, Axel. *Coco Chanel. A Biography*. London: Bloomsbury, 1990
Maire, Robert. *Mémoires en Images. Antibes Juan-Les-Pins*, Éditions Alan Sutton, 2001
Maupassant, Guy de. *Afloat*. Peter Owen Publishers, 1995
McBrien, William. *Cole Porter. The Definitive Biography*. London: Harper Collins Publishers, 1998
McReynolds, Louise. *Russia At Play. Leisure Activities at the End of the Tsarist Era*. London, Cornell University Press, 2003
Meiffret, J.B. *Guide d'Antibes et de ses Campagnes*. Nice: Faraud & Conso, 1877
Méjean Paul. *D'Antipolis à Juan-Les-Pins*. Éditions Bordas, 1969
Menegaldo, Hélène. *Les Russes à Paris, 1919-1939*. Autremont, 1998
Mewshaw, M. *Greene in Antibes*. London Magazine, 1977
Milhailovich, Alexander. *Once a Grand Duke*. New York, Garden City, 1932
Morris, Margaret. *My Life in Movement*. London, The International Association of MMM Ltd, 2003
Mrena, Andrea. *Histoire de la Colonie Russe sur la Côte d'Azur*. Agth Books, 2017
Myers, Paul A. *French Sketches: Cap d'Antibes and the Murphys*, Paul A Myers Books, 2011